CRITICAL ISSUES IN CURRICULUM
John Willinsky, EDITOR

Feminist Teaching in Theory and Practice

SITUATING POWER AND KNOWLEDGE IN POSTSTRUCTURAL CLASSROOMS

Becky Ropers-Huilman

FOREWORD BY MAGDA GERE LEWIS

Teachers College, Columbia University
New York and London

Published by Teachers College Press, 1234 Amsterdam Avenue, New York, NY 10027

A previous version of chapter 2 appeared in *Gender and Education,* 9(3) (1997), under the title "Constructing Feminist Teachers: Complexities of Identity."

A previous version of chapter 8 appeared in *Feminist Teacher,* 10(1) (1996), under the title "Still Waters Run Deep: Meanings of Silence in Feminist Classrooms."

Library of Congress Cataloging-in-Publication Data

Ropers-Huilman, Becky.
    Feminist teaching in theory and practice : situating power and
knowledge in poststructural classrooms / Becky Ropers-Huilman ;
foreword by Magda Gere Lewis.
        p.   cm.—(Critical issues in curriculum)
    Includes bibliographical references and index.
    ISBN 0-8077-3694-5 (cloth : alk. paper).—ISBN 0-8077-3693-7
(pbk. : alk. paper)
    1. Feminism—Study and teaching (Higher)—United States.
    2. Feminist theory—Study and teaching (Higher)—United States.
    I. Title. II. Series.
    HQ1426.R75   1998
    305.42′071′173—dc21   97-35310

ISBN 0-8077-3693-7 (paper)
ISBN 0-8077-3694-5 (cloth)

Printed on acid-free paper
Manufactured in the United States of America

05 04 03 02 01 00 99 98   8 7 6 5 4 3 2 1

To the women and educators in my life

Contents

Series Editor's Foreword

Becky Ropers-Huilman's book does a wonderful job of reminding us that there is no more critical issue in curriculum today than thinking through our theories of teaching. This brave book is not about teaching in theory, mind you, but teaching as the deliberate and thoughtful practice of a theory. Because, as she makes clear and convincing, teaching is always about trying to realize an ideal. An ideal, in some sense, is always about a theory of the world and how it should be, and the ideal in this case is concerned with feminist practice. We cannot stand before a class or sit with a class around a circle without a theory of what has brought us together and what we are there to achieve. This is all too obvious? Well, it remains a critical issue in teaching when it comes to changing theories, and it is not simple, I far better appreciate after reading this book, in either practice or theory.

Like the other books in the Critical Issues in Curriculum series, this is a work that takes its moment from the life of the classroom, from what is at work as student and teacher gather in the name of education, and it reaches outward to where the ideas at play in the classroom begin to run into the theories that would reframe the world at large. Professor Ropers-Huilman talks to feminist teachers and takes us into their classrooms in ways that allow us to see how theory is practiced and challenged and reworked and worked again, to see how theory is embodied or, as we might say, how it is lived.

Before taking us to where theory intersects teaching, Professor Ropers-Huilman turns to feminist work within poststructuralism, so we are well prepared for a dynamic that works back and forth, as teachers' reflections on what they are doing in the classroom help us to make sense of poststructuralism's rethinking of power relations, and as the book offers poststructural frameworks on language, knowledge, and meaning that can help teacher and reader push ahead with the difficult task of reconceiving the learning process. This book thus presents anew the theory/practice relation, and demonstrates the alternative posed by feminist teaching and by feminists teaching.

This book takes us within the critical struggle against resident theories of teaching that have held the norms of practice in their throes for so long. It speaks to how dedicated educators are working hard and by their best lights to reform the theories about gender and power on which institutions and members of society base their practices. Here are the complexities, the self-doubt and renewed inspiration, of those trying to change the theory of teaching, knowing that at some point, without that familiar theory operating in the classroom, what they are doing may no longer be recognized as teaching by those who do not yet recognize the ideals of their theory.

Professor Ropers-Huilman gives truth to theory in this work by so securely locating it within the realm of immediate experience or practice, as these feminists teach each day and as they have to think about their teaching in a way that others don't because the others are not challenging anyone's expectations with their practice. It is for this vivid sense of experience and insight that we stand indebted to this book on educational change and curriculum reform, on feminist practice and postmodern theory, as forms of teaching.

It is hard to read the book without reflecting on how the reward of following the given and timeworn is a kind of thoughtlessness; it entails an ease of practice without having the burden of justification. Only with the new does one suddenly have to carry the additional demand of articulating the otherwise unstated theory in a cycle between word and deed. Fortunately for those interested in feminist teaching, Professor Ropers-Huilman assists with this articulation, breaking the isolation that innovators often suffer, while providing a strong sense of how this teaching is struggling to achieve the goals that have always been at the heart of teaching, goals of inclusion and self-realization.

As you might gather, I would particularly recommend attending to how the text follows through the experience of these teachers in their skilled and subtle practice of theory, a practice that affords lessons on how to allow others a hearing that honors those who have spoken. As if taking her lessons well from these teachers, Professor Ropers-Huilman also honors the words of those with whom she worked. You might say that in orchestrating the voices and experiences of these educators, the author has, in effect, provided the program note that gives the music a context, a running commentary of insight and connection, so that in the voice of the one, we can always hear the many. The teachers represented here are by no means of one frame of mind, and in navigating through their stances, Professor Ropers-Huilman demonstrates her own sense of feminist teaching, one that is not insistent on a given truth, but only on hearing the otherwise unheard with an ear for the ambivalence and uncertainty of the still-emerging theory of what must be an always moving feminist position, which, like any good educator, attends to the movement of the class.

Although this play of theoried practice and practiced theory is by no means the whole of the book, I think it worth stressing the break-through quality of this affirmation of teaching as a theoretical endeavor, as the lived challenge that it does not always get credit for being. Clearly, this is a salutary instance of recognizing, reversing, and collaps-ing the dichotomy between theory and practice. This is no academic exercise in deconstruction, but one that speaks to the obvious truth we often fail to appreciate that for most of us the greatest contribution that we make to the circulation and production of knowledge, to a rethinking of the world, comes of our teaching. Professor Ropers-Huilman gives teaching the accord it warrants, as a site of reflection and production. The breathtaking realism, or grounded quality, of the book is apparent when it describes how when one teacher, Brianne, comes to consider this question of reflection, she explains with candor how she steers between what she calls making a fetish of radicalizing the organization of the course and getting on with the practical work of the course. Professor Ropers-Huilman, in turn, does not hesitate to take up the power enacted in this navigation, while paying close mind to what it means for students to engage and disengage with the resulting prac-tices.

What stands out in all of this interest in practice is how clearly the critical issue of social justice underwrites feminist teaching. It concerns how teachers "hold the power." It is worked through the teachers' handling of disruptive and resistant students in ways that always accord respect when patience would otherwise be exhausted. But it is most importantly realized in the sense of commitment to seeing this principle enacted for all students.

This is a book about teachers in the process of teaching and thinking about teaching, caught in the act, as it were, without having all of the answers by any means, but with that very spirit of inquiry, of searching, that marks the earnest and engaging moments in the best classrooms. Everywhere there are critical moments when you can feel that the peo-ple here are taking tentative steps into new regions, getting a feel for going where theory proposes and practice will affirm. Professor Ropers-Huilman captures, as does no one else I have read, the nuanced ten-sions around creating a safe environment, of fostering a learning climate that invites and recognizes difference while still allowing for the leader-ship responsibilities of the designated teacher. She captures all this by conveying the whole weight of these classroom experiences and reflections, so that one feels the tension and understands that this is the work of balancing eggs on their ends, and yet something so much more constructive and of such lasting value, with no less need for constant attention.

John Willinsky
Wm. Allen Visiting Professor, Seattle University

Foreword

In this text, Becky Ropers-Huilman reminds us that the very best teaching is that which simultaneously troubles and beckons the imagination in a context where no less is at stake than the achievement of our collective commitment to democratic citizenship and social, environmental, and economic justice. As the explosion of the knowledge and communications technologies hurls us toward the 21st century, the grip of neoconservatism and the discourse of the profit mandates of the global economy have assured us that we are headed for an era when both democracy and justice of any sort will be in short supply. As the who and how of social participation falls more and more into the hands of corporate conglomerates, the academy, itself under threat, is one of the last sites where the struggle over the agenda that articulates the instrumentalities and ideologies of everyday culture is still under debate.

History has shown us that every regime, whether reactionary or progressive, is aware of the power of education and schooling as that site where either conserving or transforming mandates are hammered into place. It is for this reason that the work teachers do with students, at whatever stage of the schooling enterprise, is a crucial site of examination and self-reflection. To the extent that feminist teachers have laid claim to this debate, Ropers-Huilman's invitation to enter some of their classrooms and to participate in the discussions of what constitutes feminist/critical teaching discourses provides an unique and welcome opportunity for anyone—teachers and students, feminist or not—interested in the question of what dynamics contribute to the possibilities of teaching for social responsibility.

In this work, Ropers-Huilman invites us into the site of debate over teaching practices that might, on the one hand, be applied to maintain or, on the other hand, be used to transform the larger social constructs and relations that schooling and education serve. Using the analytical frameworks of some of the major contemporary English-speaking scholars in the conversation about feminist pedagogy, Ropers-Huilman has pulled together the self-reflective voices of feminist teachers as they speak from inside that institution in which their presence was never anticipated. Through a systematic application of theory to practice, she has presented rich and textured documentation of the politics of education and schooling from a feminist poststructuralist perspective. And she has done this with care and respect for the daily struggles and the lived contradictions of the feminist teachers who are the participants in this ethnography.

For those of us who work, similarly, from a feminist poststructuralist teaching discourse, Ropers-Huilman invites a personal reading. For me, this reading is visceral. I connect both to the exhilaration and to the despair of teaching as a woman and as a feminist in an institutional culture that welcomes neither, yet harbors pockets of students and faculty (both women and men) whose commitment to teaching and learning for the purposes of healing and mending a scarred world cannot be bought off by promises of academic prestige and advancement. Those of us committed to a feminist/critical agenda who teach in the academy know the liabilities of a teaching practice that sets out to challenge institutional norms, structures, and knowledges. Being a feminist/critical teacher in the academy is not a career move.

Throughout Ropers-Huilman's text, we are reminded that the context we have been invited into is a postmodernist one: a moment in history when everything is up for grabs, even as the very possibility of continued life on the planet is at stake. The threat is no longer the fabricated dangers of an East/West wrestling for ideological power, but now, much more insidiously and "invisibly," the realities of a profit-driven disregard for the natural systems that maintain the very life of us all. In this regard, the voices of the teachers who participated in this study remind us that what we do in classrooms is not an "academic" exercise but the very foundation of future possibilities. The voices in this text speak powerfully to the mandates of commitment and self-reflection: feminist or not, teachers cannot renege on their responsibility in the classroom. It is in this regard that Ropers-Huilman, the teacher participants in the study, and, indeed, all of us, are called to the question, What is the relationship between teaching and social activism? What does it mean when we ask students to embrace their knowledge as a verb? What does it mean when students refuse the political implications of what their knowledge puts on offer? What are the social forces that drive what is taught and what is learned? What does it mean to put "empowerment" on the syllabus?

If the beginning of the modern era and the rise of Western industrial capitalism was signaled by a turn to scientism and the search for certainty and predictability through standardization for the purpose of achieving the democratization of civic life, then their decline is marked by the tensions of a negotiated abandonment of the pursuit of their failed promises. The academy is a central figure in these negotiations. And within the academy, those for whom it was never intended are the key protagonists, feminist teachers among them.

As a text that reveals feminist teachers' experience of the academy within a "postmodern democratic society," this is ultimately a text about power and the effects of its institutional and personal uses. This text raised questions for me both implicitly and explicitly—questions that have troubled me and with which I have deliberately troubled my own teaching: What is the reciprocity between teachers and students? What responsibilities are implied if teachers see themselves as agents of social change? If personal experience is taken to be the foundation of knowledge production and the making of meaning, where meaning-making is conversely also the lens through which experience is made sense of, how can/do feminist teachers ensure psychic/emotional/affective safety for individuals in the classroom? What are the psychic/emotional/affective effects on feminist teachers of teaching agendas that choose to disquiet, to disrupt, to make uncomfortable students' taken-for-granted notions of how the world works? What happens in the classroom when gender/racial relations of power turn institutional power structures on their head? What are the implications for feminist teachers of the fact that our commitment to feminist politics inside the classroom *requires* teaching methodologies that explicitly neutralize and efface our own institutional authority? What happens when students respond to these efforts in such a way that not only the method but the knowledge thus purveyed is, itself, considered suspect? If feminist scholarship is politics inside the academy, what are the personal/professional implications for feminist teachers of critiquing/resisting the institutions which engage us, on the one hand, and the institutionalization of feminist scholarship, on the other?

This text reminds us that the essence of feminist theory, knowledge, and teaching is the awareness of power as a dynamic in the world—that it is central to who we are and what we teach; that the pedagogical processes that are an examination of the workings of power require us to turn answers into questions; and that it is not the answers we find but the questions we pose that place knowledge, thus produced, in the service of social transformation.

To read this work prescriptively would be counter to the spirit of Ropers-Huilman's intent. It is not her intention, nor is it the intention of her research participants, to prescribe mandates for feminist teaching.

Indeed, such a reading would disregard the very real and often clearly personally difficult experiences with which the subjects of this research struggle and invite us to struggle along with them.

Rather, this work provides an insider look at the question, What is feminist teaching? It provokes us to examine our own teaching for what it implies and what it overlooks, for what it offers and what it shrinks from putting on offer, for what it intends and what it prevents. It reminds us that knowledge production resides in the crevices, the interstices, and the fault lines between competing and opposing ideologies. And finally, this work encourages us to engage with our students and colleagues in academic institutions, at all levels, with the full knowledge that in this era of neoconservatism, it is not only the what but also the how of our teaching that carries the full potential as well as the full liability for the possibilities of a politically committed democratic citizenry.

Magda Gere Lewis
Queen's University
Kingston, Canada

Preface

To establish a beginning point for this book, I want to make clear the motivations and assumptions I embraced when embarking on this project several years ago. As I prepared for this exploration, I knew that I was interested in how feminists negotiated the educational environments in which they worked. I perceived that higher education institutions, and most of the people operating within them, functioned in ways that did not embrace feminism as I defined it. With these understandings, I was seeking in feminist teachers subversive and brave pioneers who had transcended the restrictions of institutional pressures and who had created classrooms that reflected *my* feminist principles. In essence, I was looking for various models of feminist teaching from which I could learn as I crafted my practice.

I was surprised by what I found. Each of the 22 teachers whom I interviewed or observed seemed to interpret feminism and feminist teaching in different ways. Some sought to create common experiences among class members, hoping to form some sort of a community, while others emphasized various differences among participants. Some thought that it was empowering for students to require them to speak in class, while others felt that such a requirement would reinforce the dominant and sometimes oppressive role of the teacher. I resonated with the literature and experience on which some teachers based their understandings, whereas others seemed to base their practices on an agenda that felt too radical or too conservative for my tastes, often leading me to wonder in my middle-of-research panic if these people were *really* feminists. Although this concern quickly dissipated, my preconceived definition of feminism was stretched beyond its previous parameters.

The participants in this study interpreted feminist teaching in several different ways; thus, any attempt to timelessly define its common elements is problematic. At the beginning of my research, however, I believed that several concerns were common in feminist educational environments. For example, I thought that those involved in feminist teaching reflected on classroom issues related to authority, power, and truth, and the ways in which these three intermingle and inform each other. I thought that they would be committed to equity, recognizing that knowledge and power are closely related and can be used to foster equitable and inequitable relations. Further, I believed that they would seek to acknowledge the uniqueness of every educational environment.

In many cases, my preconceptions bore themselves out. Yet, I learned through this research that feminist teaching is not just one approach, practice, or tool. Instead, it is a continually reforming approach to knowing and understanding. It is largely shaped by the social forces that intersect within its boundaries. As such, I found that there was no *pure* space that I could call "feminist teaching."

My focus on feminist teaching discourse or practices, rather than only on feminist teachers, allows me to acknowledge the "impurity"— or, rather, complexity—of this conversation. Through considering and utilizing as data the experiences and understandings of feminists in teaching contexts, I am able to examine "feminist teaching" without falsely limiting the various contexts and discourses in which it exists and operates. In other words, the participants in my study maintained a complex set of identities that shaped their teaching practices. My developing understandings of feminist teaching were made both more complex and much richer because of the intersections of those identities. I claim neither that the words and actors informing this research were operating exclusively within feminist teaching discourse, nor that they all had poststructural philosophies or inclinations. Instead, they were instrumental to me in a process of constructing multiple meanings of what poststructuralism and feminism can contribute to teaching contexts. Therefore, the focus of this research remains on forces that affect feminist teaching practice or discourse and beliefs or approaches that I found to be generally associated with—and disrupted within—that discourse.

Both in terms of its possibilities for enhancing the educational experiences of teachers and students and for exploring issues commonly brought to the forefront in poststructural feminist thought (such as the influences and development of power, difference, knowledge, and language), feminist teaching provides a useful point of entry as I begin to ponder the question of how feminism shapes educational experience. Elsewhere, I have completed an overview of common themes in feminist teaching literature (Ropers-Huilman, 1996); in this study I address multiple factors that affect the practices of those who find feminist teaching discourses compelling. I further examine the ways in which those factors and practices are embedded in power relations.

Rather than focus only on specific events, I attempt to create conversations between participants in this research, voices in the literature, and my own questions and musings. Throughout the text I call attention to the places where literature, the voices or actions of research participants, and my own tendencies and beliefs "bumped" into each other and shaped the path of my research. The tentative ideas I propose in the final section expand some of the disruptions that resulted from the conversations I crafted.

In this research, I am not seeking the answer to the question, What is feminist teaching? Rather, I am creating a multifaceted vision of feminist teaching by examining social forces that continually shape its discourses, practices, and interpretations. I am further exploring new inquiries that have been, or have the potential to be, provoked by poststructural analyses of those multiple interpretations.

At least three concerns motivated this research. First, Jennifer Gore (1993) established the need for analyses of feminist teaching that move beyond descriptive, uncritical, "celebratory" sharing of strategies used in feminist classrooms (p. 31). I hope to add to previous research that discussed the struggles and contradictions involved in critical or feminist teaching practices, and the approaches understood to be useful in certain contexts (Ellsworth, 1992; Gore, 1993; Lather, 1991; Lewis, 1993; Luke & Gore, 1992a; Orner, 1992).

Second, several authors have asserted that while theory and educational strategies and understandings are closely and uniquely linked to the contexts in which they are situated, it would be useful for them as feminists and teachers to be presented with options for practice from which to choose (Bright, 1987; Bunch, 1983; Gore, 1990, 1993, 1997). Through my presentation of many philosophies and viewpoints in this work, all of which are context bound and situation specific, an array of understandings of feminist teaching provides options for practice.

Third, calls for empowerment, examinations of relationships between students and teachers, and the emphasis on action in feminist classrooms have all been considered in feminist and educational literature as interrelated parts of feminist teaching. Yet while emphasizing the interconnectedness of innumerable environmental factors and circumstances that contribute to and influence a given educational experience, several authors have raised questions about the problematic role that teachers play in feminist educational environments (Bright, 1987; Gore, 1990, 1993; Jipson, 1995; Lather, 1991; Orner, 1992). When considering feminist education, how do teachers influence and perceive social forces affecting classrooms in which they work? What are the customs or norms that guide feminist teaching practice? What are the resistances to these norms? What are the relationships between feminist teaching and other discourses? Jennifer Gore (1993) has suggested that in the search for understandings of the constructions of feminist teaching, it would be useful to direct analytical gazes toward the position of teachers. I hope to contribute multiple perspectives on feminist teaching based on my experiences with a variety of feminist educators and, in response to those perspectives, suggest further possibilities that poststructuralism suggests.

In this research, I sought multiple explanations and interpretations of what it means to engage in feminist teaching and to participate in constructing a feminist teaching discourse. In my attempts to represent what I learned about feminist teaching philosophies and the multiple teaching practices they yielded, I present my work in the following way.

After describing how this research took shape in chapter 1, I divide the work into two major parts, "Engaging Change: Social Forces and Feminist Teaching Practice" and "Engaging Power: Critical Tensions and Resistances." In "Engaging Change: Social Forces and Feminist Teaching Practice" (chapters 2, 3, and 4), I focus on the question, *What contributes to a multiplicity of forms of feminist teaching?* Through examinations of teachers' multiple identities and identity constructions (chapter 2), of the students involved as classroom participants (chapter 3), and of institutional structures and expectations (chapter 4), I examine the various ways in which these social forces shaped feminist teaching practices.

In the second section, "Engaging Power: Critical Tensions and Resistances," I turn to the question, *How does power influence constructions of feminist teaching?* Although this question is implicit throughout the research, it is at this point that I focus the analysis explicitly on power. In chapter 5, I reflect on the ways in which teachers interpreted power relations in their classrooms and educational experiences, especially regarding student resistances. In chapter 6, the multiple ways that power affected knowledge constructions become the focus. In chapter 7, I consider interpretations of difference in feminist teaching discourses and the ways in which power relations were embedded within those interpretations. In chapter 8, I focus on the ways that communication through speech and silence both demonstrated and undermined power relations. In chapters 5 through 8, I consider the implications of this research for developing a feminist poststructural teaching discourse. In the final chapter, "Intersections and Interruptions: Letting Loose with Disruption," I discuss multiple feminist teaching practices that seemed to transcend my categorical framework. I conclude with lingering questions that still provoke me as I continue to both experience and develop my own feminist teaching discourse.

Acknowledgments

Although many people have fostered my work through encouraging words and inquiries, there are a few whom I would like to acknowledge individually here. First, I thank all the participants in this research who allowed me to look closely at their practices while struggling with me to understand their meanings. I especially thank Gloria Ladson-Billings and Mary Louise Gomez, whose openness to my work contributed immeasurably to its final form.

Clif Conrad has also been instrumental to this work in many ways. Clif's urging that I consider the implications of the words that I was writing encouraged me to explore previously unconsidered and challenging opportunities. These explorations brought both me and this work closer to being what I hoped both I and it would be. Cryss Brunner has unfailingly provided me with an environment in which I feel positive energy, comfort, and confidence. Her kind words of faith coupled with her intellectual curiosity and clarity provided me with both inspiration and direction in my thinking. Liz Ellsworth, Colleen Capper, and Paul Bredeson offered additional support, each providing me with models of how to make contributions to academic communities.

I would also like to thank my family: Ray, Rosa, Kathy, Deb, and Dan Ropers, Julie Ropers-Rosendahl, and Jeff Rosendahl. These people have listened to me struggle with ''irrational'' poststructural thoughts, pondered with me the implications of feminism for how we live our lives, and encouraged me to walk along many paths of inquiry. Through their constant interest and willingness to support my passion for learning, they have strengthened my abilities to make contributions to both my academic and personal communities.

Finally, I would like to thank my partner in life, Brian Ropers-Huilman. With me, he has prioritized this project over many other opportunities. He, more than anyone else, has engaged with the intensity that feminism and poststructuralism provoke in me, both in teaching and learning situations and in our lives more broadly conceived. His passion for inquiry rivals that of anyone I know; and his respect for human integrity has my utmost admiration and appreciation. He has undoubtedly influenced both this work and my ability to complete it.

CHAPTER 1

Puzzling My Way Toward/Through Feminist Teaching

You look at where you're going and where you are and it never makes sense, but then you look back at where you've been and a pattern seems to emerge. And if you project forward from that pattern, then sometimes you can come up with something.

(Pirsig, 1974, p. 168)

Everything is contestable; nothing is off-limits; and no outcomes are guaranteed. These are the conditions of a "philosophy of praxis," which demands of its disciples that they put aside, for the time being, the rank-and-file state of mind—in other words, their willing suspension of disbelief in a fixed ethical horizon.

(Ross, 1988, p. xv)

Whereas scholars and educators have taken a variety of perspectives on a wide span of theories and pedagogical styles, the labeling of approaches as *poststructural* is a relatively recent phenomenon in higher education literature (Bloland, 1995). Various forms of the current wave of feminism have, however, been developing for many decades. I chose to approach this research from a feminist poststructural point of view, as I find that it is useful in examining the contradictory and complex positions of teachers who are engaging with/in feminist teaching. Both feminism and poststructuralism have implications for the literature I chose to review, the people I asked to participate, my methodological approaches, and the understandings I have formed through this research.

In this section, I first discuss the main tenets of poststructuralism as I have come to understand them. I then review several educational scholars' perspectives on the possibilities of combining feminist and poststructural thought, highlighting those who think that it is a useful conjoining as well as those who think that it is a combination whose

1

components are politically and theoretically opposed. Finally, I speculate on the areas of this specific research on which feminist poststructuralism could most readily focus.

POSTSTRUCTURAL CONTRIBUTIONS

Definitions and uses of poststructuralism as a philosophical or methodological approach may be slightly or radically different depending on the person who is articulating its meaning and the situation in which it is being applied. Indeed, Andrew Ross (1988) stated:

> That it has achieved such diverse cultural currency as a term thereby demonstrates what has been seen as one of postmodernism's most provocative lessons: that terms are by no means guaranteed their meanings, and that these meanings can be appropriated and redefined for different purposes, different contexts, and, more important, different causes. (p. xi)

By claiming the constant shifting of meaning depending on historical and cultural situations, consequences, and intentions, poststructuralism also necessarily problematizes the consistency and stability of its own meaning. It recognizes and seeks to address the implications and interests that are constantly present in its always situational meaning. Before proceeding, I offer a clarification of concepts that I use throughout this work.

Discourse

Discourse, the first of these concepts, is often used in poststructural theorizing to describe the many and varied influences that are acting on and being expressed in a particular situation. As Chris Weedon (1987) articulated,

> Discourses, in Foucault's work, are ways of constituting knowledge, together with the social practices, forms of subjectivity and power relations which inhere in such knowledges and the relations between them. . . . Neither the body nor thoughts and feelings have meaning outside their discursive articulation, but the ways in which discourse constitutes the minds and bodies of individuals is always part of a wider network of power relations, often with institutional bases. (p. 108)

Weedon further stated:

> Through a concept of *discourse*, which is seen as a structuring principle of society, in social institutions, modes of thought and individual subjectivity,

> feminist poststructuralism is able, in detailed, historically specific analysis,
> to explain the working of power on behalf of specific interests and to
> analyse the opportunities for resistance to it. (p. 41)

Several others have presented explanations of this term as well. In reflecting on Foucault's work, Jane Flax (1993) described three facets of
what she understood to be discourse or "discursive formations." Discourse is "historically contingent, dynamic, and conflict ridden," con-
sists of "dynamic and productive systems" that "produce knowledge,
power, and experts," and includes "rules that enable members to identify some statements as true or false" (p. 39).

Throughout this discussion, I understand *discourse* to include the
larger social forces that both influence practice and, indeed, constitute
unique discourses themselves. Within this definition, human actors
both construct and are constructed by the discourses in which they are
located. Discourse in this research, then, includes practices and philosophies, customs and norms, and attitudes and strategies of and about
feminist teaching. It is around feminist teaching discourse, rather than
feminist teachers themselves, that I center this analysis.

Poststructuralism

The second term that I introduce at this time is *poststructuralism*
itself. This concept has been criticized for being difficult both to understand and to communicate to others (Tong, 1989). While I hold that it is
not necessarily beyond understanding and application, I am mindful of
Sue Middleton's (1993) description of this somewhat elusive concept as
follows:

> I understand [poststructuralism] to mean a disbelief, skepticism, or suspen-
> sion of belief in universal truth or in the possibility of a totalizing master
> narrative and, instead, a focus on the various master narratives, disciplines,
> or theories as regimes of truth—as historical and socially constructed
> knowledge with varying and unequal relations to various apparatuses of
> power. (p. 58)

By presenting poststructuralism in this manner, Middleton provided a
way to begin conceptualizing the possibilities for application of this
philosophy or approach to specific situations or discourses, all situated
within a society that holds dearly to master narratives.

Both Dennis Carlson (1995) and Harland Bloland (1995) have asserted that there are many "strands" of postmodernism. Poststructuralism is variously presented as synonymous to, a strand of, or a philoso-

phy undergirding postmodernism. In this research, I draw primarily from work associated with Michel Foucault and conceptualize post-structuralism as an approach to knowing. I hope to further clarify my uses and understandings of poststructuralism in the discussions below as I articulate what are, in my mind, some of its most useful concepts. I discuss each of these concepts individually; I also, however, seek to articulate overlaps and links between them, and urge the reader to do so as well. I end each section with a set of questions that serve as a starting point for poststructural analyses.

Power

A conceptual focal point in poststructural thought is that which problematizes and attempts to locate sources and uses of power. Foucault (1978) stated many characteristics of his conceptualization of power as used in his analyses. First, he suggested that "power is exercised from innumerable points, in the interplay of nonegalitarian and mobile relations" (p. 94). Power is not something that is able to be grasped and held on to by people who have somehow found themselves at the top of a hierarchical system. Rather, power passes through and is exercised by persons and structures at all levels in all social systems. Second, Foucault believed that power relations have directly productive, rather than merely repressive, roles in social systems whenever and wherever they are exercised. Those productive roles are not merely exterior considerations, but rather are inherent in all conditions. Third, he submitted that there is no truly existing duality between those "with power" and those "without power." Social systems have changed and are constantly changing as a result of shifting power relations within their structures. Therefore, any attempt to delineate clear and firm lines of who has and doesn't have power will be both incomplete and situation-bound. Fourth, he stated that power is always exercised with aims and objectives. Yet, at the same time, he cautioned that this does not mean that a "subject" is making choices about and planning those objectives. Rather, he suggested:

> The rationality of power is characterized by tactics that are often quite explicit at the restricted level where they are inscribed . . . tactics which, becoming connected to one another, attracting and propagating one another, but finding their base of support and their condition elsewhere, end by forming comprehensive systems: the logic is perfectly clear, the aims decipherable, and yet it is often the case that no one is there to have invented them, and few who can be said to have formulated them. (p. 95)

Foucault further suggested that power is always coexistent with resistance, not as an outside force, but as an integral part of power itself.

Several feminist authors have focused on Foucault's conceptualization of power as integral to poststructuralism. Patti Lather (1991) linked power relations to language, suggesting that definition or description of persons, constructs, or structures serves to inscribe meaning on a given entity, rather than to describe its essence. In other words, *description* is laden with contextual implications of the person or text that is describing and, therefore, marks those whose meaning has been articulated as having certain relations with privilege and power. Mimi Orner (1992) emphasized the usefulness of language examination as well, stating, "It is crucial that we see how the terms interrelate, how they have been historically constructed as opposites, and how they have been used to justify and naturalize power relations" (p. 78). Language is closely related to power relations in poststructural approaches.

In turning their analyses on themselves, poststructural thinkers have questioned the power relations that are inherent in their own adoption of poststructuralism. Andrew Ross (1988), for example, queried:

> If we accept nonetheless, at the largest philosophical level of the debate, that the political status of claims to universality is at stake, then the following question ought to be addressed. In whose interests is it, exactly, to declare the abandonment of universals? For it is here that we may face the ethical question of postmodernism, a question about its political "horizon" (or lack thereof). (p. xiv)

Ross further suggested that poststructuralism has created a new understanding and conceptualization of difference and power that has the potential to create and uphold new structures through which inequality can operate. Fortunately, poststructuralism allows for a critique of its own situatedness and constructedness, of its own premises and assumptions, as well as of those of other theoretical approaches. In other words, it recognizes itself as an approach which has developed in a specific time and place, with certain motivations and intentions (Best & Kellner, 1991; Ross, 1988). The critiques that poststructuralism suggests for other theories and philosophies are therefore able to be utilized to expand and reconstruct the primary and "fundamental" tenets of poststructuralism itself.

Poststructuralism, as any theory, can be seen as a totalizing and destructive force that serves only those who have created or learned how to manipulate it. It can also, however, be seen as a productive force that can help us to understand differently the social interactions in which we participate both as observers and participants. In this sense, it is best seen as a potential tool for understanding—one that has the ability both to build up and break down rigid social structures.

In my understanding, a poststructural epistemology would lead to a methodology in which questions concerning power would be loosely based on the themes outlined above. For example, what are the points or sources through which power is currently being exercised? How are those in all levels of a traditional hierarchy exercising power? What are the aims and objectives of existing power relations? What are the points or sources of resistance to these power relations? What are power relations producing? And finally, what alternative structures and potential sources of oppression are being produced by shifting power relations?

Knowledge and Meaning

Another central tenet of poststructuralism involves conceptualizing knowledge and inscribing meaning. In poststructuralism, knowledge is thought to be partial and political; power and knowledge coexist in their enactments and effects (Gore, 1993). Knowledge that is viewed as complete and true in a given social context varies over time, and those whose knowledge is most highly regarded in any such context are often defined as those with the greatest power. Legitimized knowledge in poststructuralism changes depending on the context and the power relations in a given context. Additionally, the legitimized knowledge that certain discourses support is able to be articulated and deconstructed.

Since meaning and knowledge will always be flexible and partial (Ross, 1988; Weedon, 1987), as well as constantly shaped by the historical and social contexts in which we are situated (Lather, 1991), meaning can be understood to be inscribed *on* given entities, rather than objectively described *about* them. In Foucault's words (cited in Gore, 1993), "'Truth' is linked in circular relation with systems of power which produce and sustain it, and to effects of power which it induces and which extend it" (p. 55). Meaning shifts depending on the social, historical, and political forces that are, in a specific situation, crafting multiple interpretations for its various observers.

While poststructuralism doesn't attempt to negate the possibility of reality, it attempts to illuminate how our perceptions of that reality are constantly grounded in the shifting social systems in which we are operating. As Lather (1991) expressed it, "Rather than dismissing 'the real,' postmodernism foregrounds how discourses shape our experience of 'the real' in its proposal that the way we speak and write reflects the structures of power in our society'' (p. 25). In poststructuralism, ideological processes and power relations that shape the meanings we ascribe to the world around us (as well as to ourselves) are "precarious, contradictory and in process'' (Weedon, 1987, p. 33). Poststructuralism suggests that any attempts we make to establish objective truths and timeless realities will be at best partial, and at worst dangerous.

From this poststructural epistemology, I interpret the methodological questions that aid in analyses of knowledge and meaning as being situation or discourse specific. They lead me to ask, in a particular situation or discourse, at a particular time, what knowledge is most readily validated? Who, or what structures, are in positions of validation? What are the resistances to existing knowledges? What are the competing knowledge sources? How are they validated? How are they enacted? What are the power relations that enable a certain knowledge to be accepted and validated within a given discourse? How does meaning ascribed to key variables within a discourse change depending on situational or historical contexts?

Language

Analysis of communication through language also holds a central place in poststructural thought. As we choose and use the language available to us, the parameters of our expression shape our thoughts and understandings. As such, language is closely related to poststructural perspectives on both power and knowledge. The tentativeness and partiality of meanings in legitimated knowledge, as well as the constant shifting of power relations within social systems, lead to a language which is also tentative, partial, and constantly shifting. Weedon (1987) suggested that "meaning is produced within language rather than reflected by language, and . . . individual signs do not have intrinsic meaning but acquire meaning through the language chain and their difference within it from other signs'' (p. 23). Weedon's analysis further claimed that it is primarily by using language as a vehicle for enactment of power, knowledge, and meaning that we communicate, produce, and reproduce the constantly changing structures of our social systems.

Mimi Orner (1992) supported Weedon's view when she contended that language can never fully represent anything or anyone. And Harland Bloland (1995) concurred: "For Derrida [also considered to be a poststructural thinker], the meanings of words are permanently in flux. Word meanings continually escape their boundaries as these meanings are negotiated and renegotiated in social settings'' (p. 526). Somewhere between the articulation of meaning and the presence of reality, in poststructural thought, lies a chasm whose essence is not able to be communicated through the language that we currently use, construct, and understand.

From a poststructural epistemology, then, language as a unit of analysis would suggest the following questions: What language is being used to express validation? What language is being used to express resistance? How is silence, the absence of language, used for communication? How is language challenged and changed? Who holds a stake in changing or retaining existing language patterns or styles? How is power communicated through language? What discourses are available for the communication of meaning? What technology is used to communicate meaning and power? Which voices or stories find outlets for expression? Which are considered unimportant?

Difference

A final key tenet within poststructural discourses that I discuss here is that of difference. Closely related to the ways in which power, knowledge, and language are appropriated in poststructuralism, the concept of difference seeks to address both the relations between a variety of differences and power, and the dualisms that are found within Western rationalist thinking. A poststructural analysis of difference further illustrates how those dualisms are rife with power investments as they relate to knowledge and meaning validation. Poststructuralism also points out that these dualisms are communicated through language and discourses that instate and reinstate, construct and maintain, social structures created by those investments.

As communicated regularly through discourse, these dualisms have important implications for the ways in which we think and act that are not entirely clear. Joan Wallach Scott (1990) asserted, "Fixed oppositions conceal the extent to which things presented as oppositional are, in fact, interdependent" (p. 137). That is, the existence and current meaning of one term is only understood in relation to its component part in a pair. That pairing, however, is problematic in that the first term is understood as the primary term, and the second term is understood as the absence or negation of the first. The acceptance of these dualisms as "common sense" without problematizing the power relations that they establish is a concern of those engaging with poststructural thought. In turn, many poststructural thinkers attempt to expose the dualisms that have been commonly accepted in Western thinking in order to clarify and, often, deconstruct their underlying assumptions.

As a theory that attempts to illuminate and expose power statuses that are inherent in both primary and secondary positions in dualisms, poststructuralism has the potential to serve those who have consistently occupied that secondary or "Other" status. As Andrew Ross (1988) suggested,

> Postmodern politics has been posed as a politics of difference, wherein many of the voices of color, gender, and sexual orientation, newly liberated from the margins, have found representation under conditions that are not exclusively tailored to the hitherto heroicized needs and interests of White, male intellectuals and/or White, male workers. (p. xvi)

While he pointed out that poststructuralism's potential should be embraced with caution because of the possibilities of setting up new systems of oppression and domination, Ross nevertheless addressed its usefulness for those who have been constructed and placed on the margins of social systems.

Within research or analysis, a poststructural epistemology grapples with the concept of difference in many ways. Its questions may include, Which dualisms are at play in a given discourse? What power relations do they establish and maintain? Who or what is the primary being and who or what is relegated to secondary status? In other words, who is considered as the Other? How do those individuals accept or resist those acquired statuses? What is at stake in our quest for difference or commonality? Which differences are seen as relevant? Which are seen as unimportant?

CRITICISMS OF POSTSTRUCTURALISM

As expressed above, the interplay of these themes creates a philosophical approach that is shifting and situational. Consequently, the application of poststructuralism in examining social contexts has, like all approaches, potentially negative consequences for those who choose to implement it or view, construct, and understand their world through its lens. For example, Patti Lather (1991) suggested that there are at least three drawbacks to poststructuralism. In her view, poststructuralism may foster an inattention to the massively uneven distribution of wealth (and, I would add, opportunity) in current social structures. Since the focus is on specific and unique contexts, poststructural analyses may neglect large-scale social trends that differentially affect its members. Lather further warned of a danger of collapsing specific groups or concepts into a "generalized otherness" that eventually negates the diversity and difference existing within or between those groups. Finally, she posited that poststructural discourse is not readily accessible to groups and individuals existing on the margins, even though it is at least partly these persons for whom poststructuralism is intended.

Jennifer Gore (1993) extended Lather's criticism to include and critique the use of poststructural thought for educational analyses. While supporting the use of poststructural approaches to analyses of educational interactions because "much of the education production of knowledge takes place at the very private, personal level of the teacher and student, and therefore cannot all be explained (away) with structuralism or structuralist politics" (p. 49), Gore also realized that it may have its drawbacks. Because of poststructuralism's constant awareness of the specificity of contextualized meaning, it may have limited theoretical use for those who try to generalize its meanings to their particular situations.

Further, Harland Bloland (1995) suggested that while there are many types of postmodernism, a "hardcore postmodernism" not only delegitimates modernism without offering solutions, but also has the potential to re-create dangerous hierarchies: "The result [of hardcore postmodernism] will again be hierarchy, but without the values of merit, neutrality, or objectivity. It will be based strictly on power" (p. 543).

An additional limitation of the use of poststructuralism is directly related—and seemingly directly opposed—to the concept of individual agency that many feminist discourses insist upon. Carol Nicholson (1995) proposed that

> postmodernism in education entails neoconservatism in politics. Students who are taught that there is no rational way to justify political change are in effect being told to accept the status quo, an attitude that is ultimately stultifying to thought. Feminists opposed to postmodernism emphasize the need to give students ideals to live for, principles to live by, and a vision of a better future that they can help to achieve. (p. 84)

And Linda Alcoff (1988) suggested:

> The idea here [in poststructuralism] is that we individuals really have little choice in the matter of who we are, for as Derrida and Foucault like to remind us, individual motivations and intentions count for nil or almost nil in the scheme of social reality. We are constructs—that is, our experience of our very subjectivity is a construct mediated by and/or grounded on a social discourse beyond (way beyond) individual control. (p. 268)

Alcoff's and Nicholson's concerns are particularly problematic in the use of poststructural approaches. However, because poststructuralism itself claims that meaning is a continually shifting construct, it holds itself as constantly available for redefinition and, subsequently, for alternative purposes. Feminism appropriates and modifies poststructural approaches for its own purposes. Feminist poststructuralism may therefore be seen as a tool for analysis, rather than as an all-encompassing theoretical truth.

FEMINIST INTERSECTIONS WITH POSTSTRUCTURAL THOUGHT

One solution to the limitations of poststructural thought expressed above is to combine its main tenets with a theory that gives it an "action" base. Just as poststructural meaning shifts and is flexible over time, so have the various feminisms grown and changed. Yet through those many changes, feminism has retained a commitment to being political and action oriented. In this section, then, I do not want to convey an objective and static feminist poststructuralism; I will attempt, rather, to describe how a poststructuralism that, some would claim, insists on the inability of individual agency and political action can be effectively combined with feminism, a philosophical viewpoint built on the opposite of that premise. I will also explicate the conditions in which these two philosophies trouble and interrupt each other in this research. Their premises may not always be able to be reconciled. As Peter McLaren and Colin Lankshear (1993) suggested, in a postmodern era "theorists will have to become discursive cross-dressers, always probing their own 'secret heart' that undercuts the politics they are attempting to construct" (p. 410). In cases of philosophical or theoretical conflict, I chose to proceed with one or the other's guidance, often settling on a piecemeal amalgamation of the two.

As I did previously with poststructuralism, I suggest here a tentative and "working" definition of feminism. To reiterate my prior beliefs, this is not meant to be a timeless and accurate definition. For the purposes of this work, however, I define feminism as follows: Feminist thinkers and actors believe in equality. They recognize that women and men in a wide variety of situations have not experienced equality in either public or personal relationships. More recently, feminists have also recognized that many other groups of individuals share a marginalized status, one that relegates them to positions "outside" the norm. As a result, feminism today is a philosophy that seeks equality for women as well as other oppressed persons.

While this definition of feminism may capture the beliefs of many feminists, it has also left many out. Throughout my writing of this definition, questions continually challenged my thoughts. What is equality? Why is that valued? Are public and private different? How? The term *women* as defined by some in the feminist movement has not always been inclusive of women who were not middle class, White, and heterosexual. I believe strongly that feminism has multiple meanings and multiple participants, each with its own strengths, weaknesses, and purposes. While complex, it is the wide diversity of perspectives fueling feminism that contributes to its strength and broad application.

Many thinkers have wrestled with the difficult conjoining of feminism and poststructuralism. Some have come to the (often tentative and conditional) conclusion that the two philosophies can be useful to one another (Fraser & Nicholson, 1988; Lather, 1991; Nicholson, 1989; Sawicki, 1991; Scott, 1990; Weedon, 1987). A common approach, while advocating the usefulness of this merger in scholarship and thought, is to present conditions under which such a pairing would be appropriate or useful.

Nancy Fraser and Linda Nicholson (1988) suggested that although theory as a part of poststructural feminism is not "self-contradictory," it must be a theory with specific parameters. It must be "explicitly historical, attuned to the cultural specificity of different societies and periods and to that of different groups within societies and periods" (p. 101). In this sense, it must avoid universalizing claims in the construct of gender as well as in other areas of analysis. A poststructural feminist theory, then, would take into consideration the varying social constructs that comprise each person's individual identity, rather than collapsing all of those characteristics into the generic category of *woman*.

Also advocating for the coming together of feminism and poststructuralism, Joan Wallach Scott (1990) explained how poststructuralism may best fit feminism's theoretical needs:

> We need theory that can analyze the workings of patriarchy in all its manifestations—ideological, institutional, organizational, subjective—accounting not only for continuities but also for change over time. We need theory that will let us think in terms of pluralities and diversities rather than of unities and universals. We need theory that will break the conceptual hold, at least, of those long traditions of (Western) philosophy that have systematically and repeatedly construed the world hierarchically in terms of masculine universals and feminine specificities. We need theory that will enable us to articulate alternative ways of thinking about (and thus acting upon) gender without either simply reversing the old hierarchies or confirming them. And we need theory that will be useful and relevant for

political practice. . . . It seems to me that the body of theory referred to as poststructuralism best meets all these requirements. (p. 134)

In this sense, Scott advocated that feminist scholars should exploit the likeness that poststructuralism and feminism share in their "self-conscious critical relationship to established philosophical and political traditions" (p. 135). In her mind, at the present time, poststructuralism has much to offer feminism.

In contrast, other scholars have pointed out inherent contradictions in the two theories, proposing points of contention that must be addressed before feminism and poststructuralism can be usefully united as tools of analysis or thought (Alcoff, 1988; Nicholson, 1995; Tong, 1989). A primary critique of postmodern feminist theory is its inaccessibility to the majority of persons for whom it was intended. As Rosemarie Tong pointed out, poststructural feminism may be seen as a "feminism for academicians" (p. 231). The language used in examining and analyzing situations poststructurally may be prohibitive to those who have not been introduced to important constructs in poststructural thought.

A further critique is that assumptions regarding constant and shifting difference underlying poststructuralism may preclude the development of a feminist community. Linda Alcoff (1988) presented one of her primary dilemmas for feminists contemplating the use or adoption of poststructural theory as follows: "How can we ground a feminist politics that deconstructs the female subject? Nominalism threatens to wipe out feminism itself" (p. 271). She further questioned:

> If gender is simply a social construct, the need to and even the possibility of a feminist politics becomes immediately problematic. What can we demand in the name of women if "women" do not exist and demands in their name simply reinforce the myths that they do? How can we speak out against sexism as detrimental to the interests of women if the category is a fiction? (p. 272)

Supporting the potential benefits of this combining, however, Tong (1989) recognized the importance of incorporating difference within the category of women and said, "Difference will not disappear simply because postmodern feminism stops reminding us about it" (p. 233). Jana Sawicki (1991) asserted that attention to differences within feminist communities may be beneficial to the various goals and purposes of the individuals within those communities. She articulated the possibilities for Foucault's politics of difference thus:

I have called Foucault's politics a politics of difference because it does not assume that all differences can be bridged. Neither does it assume that difference must be an obstacle to effective resistance. Indeed, in a politics of difference, difference can be a resource insofar as it enables us to multiply the sources of resistance to particular forms of domination and to discover distortions in our understandings of each other and the world. (p. 28)

She asserted further:

What is certain is that our differences are ambiguous; they may be used either to divide us or to enrich our politics. If we are not the ones to give voice to them, then history suggests that they will continue to be either misnamed and distorted, or simply reduced to silence. (p. 32)

Feminist discourses can benefit from the many strengths and perspectives of members in various communities. Poststructuralism's focus on acknowledging and understanding differences may increase the potential of these benefits.

Alcoff (1988) offered a further critique of the merger of feminist and poststructural thought. She argued, "In their defense of a total construction of the subject, post-structuralists deny the subject's ability to reflect on the social discourse and challenge its determinations" (p. 269). Alcoff raised this concern in terms of individual and group agency. How can we act within a theory that constructs us only as a product of social factors over which we ultimately have no control? Further, a theory that insists on differences and the absence of unifying structures problematizes the ability of a politics that, many would claim, focuses on gender as one of those structures.

In an attempt to address some of these very difficult questions, many scholars have insisted that feminist poststructuralism has the potential to be particularly useful in political spheres (Fraser & Nicholson, 1988; Lather, 1991; Sawicki, 1991; Scott, 1990). The attempts of some feminist scholars to break down traditional, universalized notions about social constructs and, especially in recent years, to give careful attention to the differences that exist within any given social category, are aided by poststructuralism's focus on the specificities of constantly fluctuating power relations in society. Poststructuralism's focus on differences and tentativeness is aided by feminism's attention to political action. Used as a tool to break down or deconstruct binary relationships, poststructural feminism illuminates, and allows for the analysis of, infinite points of intersection of our social structures.

Poststructural feminism does not claim that we have total control over our position in life; yet it advocates that we can recognize, and choose to act within, the social constructs that have helped to create the positions that we currently hold. As Foucault (1977/1988b) pointed out, "As soon as there is a power relation, there is a possibility of resistance. We can never be ensnared by power: we can always modify its grip in determinate conditions and according to a precise strategy" (p. 123). Chris Weedon (1987) highlighted this aspect of the debate when she insisted that those advocating feminist poststructural approaches could create space for individual agency and consciousness. In her words,

> In all poststructural discourses, subjectivity and rational consciousness are themselves put into question. We are neither the authors of the ways in which we understand our lives, nor are we unified rational beings. For feminist poststructuralism, it is language in the form of conflicting discourses which constitutes us as conscious thinking subjects and enables us to give meaning to the world and to act to transform it. (p. 32)

She emphasized further a premise that has been advocated in other areas of feminism—the freedom to be "theoretically promiscuous" (Middleton, 1993, p. 42) in choosing tools for political use. As Weedon stated, "In poststructural feminism, we can choose between different accounts of reality on the basis of their social implications" (p. 29). While touting the merits of feminist poststructuralism in her work, she simultaneously acknowledged that it is neither the final nor the only answer for feminism's theoretical concerns. There are assumptions within poststructuralism that do not resonate with every type of feminist thought. When those assumptions contradict, there will be questions that may be more appropriately addressed in other discourses or frameworks. I do not disagree with this claim, nor have I encountered any feminist poststructural thinker who has explicitly articulated her disagreement.

Feminist Poststructuralism's Implications for Research

> There is always the possibility (and actuality) of a gap, of misinterpretation, of misrecognition when we try to make sense of our relation to others. We can never be certain of the meaning of others' responses. We can never be certain of the meaning of our own responses.
>
> (Orner, 1992, p. 84)

Both feminism and poststructuralism have implications for the methods and assumptions that scholars choose to adhere to in research. My efforts to conjoin feminism and poststructuralism, as well as to

articulate places of disharmony between the two, also have such implications. In this section, I will discuss the ways in which these two
approaches can affect research, first focusing briefly on feminism and
poststructuralism individually and then shifting for the larger part of
the discussion to complexities associated with the coming together of
the two. Finally, I will discuss possibilities of theoretical construction
within feminist poststructural analyses.

Feminism in research. As in any other philosophical approach chosen for research, there are underlying assumptions in feminist research.
For example, even when the focus is not specifically on differences or
similarities between the genders, "feminist researchers see gender as a
basic organizing principle which profoundly shapes/mediates the concrete conditions of our lives" (Lather, 1991, p. 71; see also Bunch, 1983).
Feminist researchers are constantly open to the possibility (and the
probability) that gender is playing a significant role in the relations that
exist at any particular moment. They do not end their analyses by looking solely at gender, however. They also seek to understand variations
and deviations from the normative within other groups, such as race,
class, sexuality, and disability. They begin their investigations aware of
their statuses in a society that positions each of us as both oppressed
and oppressors (Weiler, 1988). Feminist researchers further draw on
lived experiences, rather than merely on abstractions or "objective"
knowledge bases, to create guidelines or theories that are useful politically to feminist movement (Acker, 1987; Weiler, 1988). As Frances
Maher (1987) described it, "Feminist methodology thus challenges the
ideals of universality and objectivity, not only because they are impossible to achieve, but because they are not useful in capturing the complexity and variety of human experience" (p. 188).

Poststructuralism in research. Shifting briefly to poststructuralism,
the guidelines and emphases for conducting research using this philosophical approach are somewhat different from those articulated above.
Michel Foucault (1978) provided four main tenets or assumptions that
undergird poststructural research. Although applied in this case to the
history of sexuality, these guidelines can be modified slightly to accommodate a variety of other situations as well. He cautioned against strict
application, however, as "these are not intended as methodological
imperatives; at most they are cautionary prescriptions" (p. 98). First,
Foucault suggested that within a discourse, a researcher should not
assume that there is an area of purity that is untouched by social and

historical contexts. Every aspect of every discourse has been modified or affected in large part by the contexts that shape social systems. Second, a researcher should not focus attention only on the duality of those with power and those without. Rather, the focus should acknowledge and take into account the multiple power relations that exist in any situation. Third, research should look not only at specificities of tactics, but also at the strategies or philosophies that continually interact with those tactics. Foucault argued that neither comes first nor is prominent; both are shaped by the other. Finally, he believed that the discourses that come into play in a given situation need to be viewed as interactive: "We must not imagine a world of discourse divided between accepted discourse and excluded discourse, or between the dominant discourse and the dominated one; but as a multiplicity of discursive elements that can come into play in various strategies" (p. 100).

In keeping with poststructural thought on power relations and on knowledge and meaning as constantly fluctuating, Lather (1991) suggested that poststructural research is also an "enactment of power relations; the focus is on the development of a mutual, dialogic production of a multi-voice, multi-centered discourse" (p. 112). Thus the focus of poststructural research is not on "finding objective answers," but rather on coming to understand differently knowledges and situations that are already assumed to be tentative, partial, and relational.

Harmonies and cacophonies in research. Feminist poststructuralism has much to offer a discussion on research methodology. As Patti Lather (1991) claimed, "A politicized postmodernism shifts the debate to a questioning of what it means to know and be known, how and why discourse works to legitimize and contest power, and the limitations of totalizing systems and fixed boundaries" (p. 88). Some feminists have chosen to grasp the potential usefulness of poststructural approaches, and have thus created a politically charged feminist poststructuralism.

In a lengthy articulation of the possibilities of using both feminism and poststructuralism in analyses, Chris Weedon (1987) argued that subjectivity is crucial for understanding women's realities. Yet poststructuralism questions the existence of subjectivities, rather than of socially formed constructions, in our lives. The poststructuralism that Weedon embraced includes room for individuals to participate in and become an inherent piece of the social processes that are constantly forming both us as subjective individuals and the society in which we operate. Resistance coexists with power; and agency coexists with discursively formed subjects. Some feminists recognize poststructural beliefs about knowledge, power, and language to be particularly useful in understanding their experiences. Consequently, they have been able to utilize it as a theory of agency as well.

Positioning Myself

> Making sense is seldom a casual exercise; we struggle to make sense in order to make our world different, to make ourselves different.
>
> (Tappan & Packer, 1991)

A key element in this, as in any, research is choosing processes through which analysis will be conducted. Before proceeding to explicate the choices that I have made, I feel it necessary to position myself as a key element in this research. I urge readers to acknowledge my various positions when grappling with the text while simultaneously questioning the effects that those positions may have had on the choices presented here and on my understandings of the participants included in this study.

I am a White woman who comes from a middle-class background in a small rural community in the midwestern United States. For most of the past 10 years, I have been involved with higher education on a relatively consistent basis in humanities- and education-related fields. As a teaching assistant, research assistant, residence hall director, and student, I have experienced many educational settings whose environmental conditions varied widely. Although I remember arguing vehemently in high school that gender need not be a barrier to achievement, I wasn't formally introduced to feminism as a political and intellectual approach until I arrived at my doctoral institution, the University of Wisconsin. My introduction to poststructuralism came at approximately the same time, although it wasn't until years later that I came to understand that it too had potential to be personally useful as an analytical and strategic device.

I bring many preconceived understandings to this work. I believe that education as it currently stands is a powerful tool for producing and reproducing culture, for guaranteeing extensive exposure to "appropriate" concepts and behaviors and, in some cases, for ensuring indoctrination. I believe that we are all variously instruments and products acting and reacting within those parameters. In this sense, feminist teaching, when located in institutions of higher education, is dangerously close to forces that ensure that we all remain within prescribed limits of functioning. In some cases, then, what is claimed to be feminist teaching can serve to be no more than traditional education with a content that is perhaps more recently developed.

I also believe that feminist teaching can offer something beyond mere exposure to key concepts and beyond just the reproduction of dominant culture. The combining of feminism and education has the potential to be subversive—encouraging not just "exposure" to concepts, but participation in experiences that could change participants' perspectives. This combination can encourage awareness that a dominant culture exists while pushing for an understanding of the subcultures that resist and support it. Feminist education has the potential to foster a hope that it is possible to create new cultures and new futures. In feminist classrooms, teachers and students can examine and enact strategies toward that end.

I believe that as higher education communities around the world grow increasingly diverse, feminist teaching provides options for teachers and administrators as they seek to educate and encourage respectful communities grounded in difference. Yet, I struggle with my own words here for several reasons. First, I do not believe that all those in higher education communities are truly interested in exploring the potential benefits that diversity has to offer. Second, my choice of words here, hoping for a *grounding* in *difference,* seems almost paradoxical. Can we achieve stability, or be grounded, in our own and each other's differences?

My exploration into the joining of feminisms and educational theories and philosophies has several important implications. I believe in the necessity of looking at feminist approaches as they can be applied in educational settings. Although feminism is not the panacea for all that ails higher education, it is a paradigmatic choice available to educators so they may examine it and subsequently determine its merits for their own situations. Further, within feminism, there are often questions that arise as to the propriety of the theories and strategies being posited as "empowering," "women-centered," and "feminist." In this sense, I am convinced that feminism has much to offer education and its participants. I am also convinced, however, that it has the potential to develop serious and harmful consequences if applied and promoted uncritically. I hope that this work will direct critical attention to feminism in education and contribute to an acknowledgment of feminist teaching as a potentially powerful educational medium. Simultaneously, I hope this work will continually deconstruct commonly accepted boundaries of feminist teaching.

Throughout the designing of this research, I operated from the assumption that it is important for feminist teaching to be approached and understood through listening to and observing those who in some way were identified as seeking to combine feminism and education as they reflected on and engaged in teaching. I wanted to participate in providing a forum where both the truths of these teachers as well as my own truths based on understandings from this research could be expressed. These beliefs about feminist teaching no doubt influenced my choice to examine feminist teaching as well as the way in which I proceeded in doing so.

Positioning the Others

> What we are about is re-metaphoring the world. We need as many and various perceivers as possible to mix metaphors wildly enough so we will never be short of them, never have to push one beyond its limits, just for lack of another to take up where it left off.
>
> (Frye, 1992a, p. 70)

A much more detailed description of my methodological choices is presented elsewhere (Ropers-Huilman, 1996); here I believe it is useful to describe the people who participated in this research as interviewees or who opened up their classrooms to me. Based on recommendations from professors and students in various departments at the University of Wisconsin, I contacted and set up interviews with 22 people in the School of Education and the Women's Studies Department, each of whom was considered by at least one colleague to be a feminist teacher. I also indicated to those who were recommending potential participants that I would like to include persons coming from diverse backgrounds and with diverse perspectives, as long as they fit the above criteria, in order to contribute to a literature and academic context that, some have claimed, has silenced certain voices.

I then developed a flexible interview protocol which focused on issues such as power and control, difference, communication, and conceptualization of knowledge, all of which are key concepts in poststructural thought. During the 22 interviews, each lasting between 50 and 90 minutes, I also asked for further recommendations from the interviewees. Following the interviews, I presented interviewees with written transcripts of our discussions. I then asked them to review their transcripts, answering any additional questions I had posed, clarifying thoughts, and adding further perspectives if so inclined. While not everyone elected to respond to this request, those who did often provided expansions of their previous understandings. These interviews constituted the first level of the research.

I choose here to provide some demographic information about the teachers who participated in this work, although I do not believe that these categories are static or determining. I do this because, as seen in my explorations on identity, both the literature and the teachers themselves asserted that these characteristics influenced the ways in which they were able to enact feminist teaching. Of the 22 teachers I interviewed, approximately 10 were over 45 years old, 8 were between 35 and 45, and 4 were under 35. Three teachers were African American, 1 was Asian American, 1 was Hispanic, and 17 were Caucasian. Five teachers were classified by the institution as instructors, 7 as assistant professors, 2 as associate professors, and 8 as full professors. Finally, 21 of the 22 research participants were women. (To preserve confidentiality among participants, I use female pronouns exclusively.) I learned from the research that many teachers believed these characteristics played a part in shaping their practices. However, other characteristics and beliefs that I discuss throughout this work influenced teachers' practices as well.

For the second level of research, I focused on two professors, from the original pool of participants, who used feminist teaching and spent more time becoming familiar with their teaching philosophies and strategies as well as with the conditions that contribute to their fluctuation. The criteria that I used for the participants in the second level were as follows: First, the teacher had to be willing to be observed through the course of a semester in a classroom situation. In conjunction with that agreement was the willingness to meet with me at various times throughout the semester. Second, teachers in this level of the research had to be reflective about their teaching. I believed that such teachers would be better aware of the contradictions and complexities inherent in their espousal of certain educational philosophies. I acknowledge that these criteria were neither "objective" nor static; however, I believe that they served to provide a (broad) useful guideline in choosing participants for the second level of this research. The two professors who worked with me in the second level of my research agreed to be named in this work; all other names are pseudonyms.

The two teachers who agreed to work with me throughout the semester were Mary Louise Gomez and Gloria Ladson-Billings, both teachers in the Department of Curriculum and Instruction at the University of Wisconsin-Madison. Each of these teachers has written extensively about her own and others' teaching practices. Further, I received at least four recommendations from colleagues in Curriculum and Instruction and other departments who claimed that my research on feminist teaching could benefit from engagement with Gloria and Mary Louise. Throughout my time with them, I found this to be the case for many reasons. First, while both of these teachers were reflective about their teaching, they enacted that reflection differently in the classes that I attended. This led me to question the multiple possibilities for feminists teaching in higher education classrooms. Second, while neither Gloria nor Mary Louise expressed that her primary self-identification would have been as a feminist teacher, each of them had explored the possibilities and problems of that characterization. My thoughts and questions were thereby multiplied by our interactions. Finally, Mary Louise and Gloria both demonstrated a passion and compassion for the struggles involved in learning to teach. Perhaps for these reasons, they gave willingly of their time and opened their classrooms so that I could engage in struggle as well.

In this second level of this research, I was a participant-observer of the teaching philosophies and strategies that Gloria and Mary Louise chose to employ in their classrooms. With students aware of the additional role that I was playing, I participated in discussions and completed assignments and readings as did they. I relied heavily on cues from the interviews in the first phase of research, as well as on the questions that I posed when discussing poststructural tenets earlier in this work, to develop an approach for understanding and recording these classroom interactions. Further, I gathered class materials such as syllabi, outside readings and suggested activities, and assignments so that I could create a more informed understanding of teachers' philosophies and strategies as well as the conditions that contribute to a variety of forms and styles of feminist teaching. I also used as sources of data solicited comments from students who participated in the classrooms that I was observing. I observed, in addition to these in-depth participant-observations, six further classrooms from one to two times as a way to increase my exposure to a variety of feminist teaching techniques and philosophies as they were enacted in classrooms.

A further analysis incorporating the perspectives of those using feminist teaching in other disciplines would be warranted; I chose to focus here, however, on teachers associated or affiliated with the Women's Studies Program or the School of Education because I believed that teachers in these locations would be more likely to have reflected on the possibilities of combining feminist and educational theories. I anticipate that the understandings from this study will nevertheless be able to inform, to various degrees, teachers in other disciplines who are able to construct parallels between the experiences communicated in this study and their own specific situations.

PART I

Engaging Change: Social Forces and Feminist Teaching Practice

What I'm coming to understand about poststructuralism is that it is a philosophy in which people are presumed not to be primarily shaped or constructed by looking at or seeking a place in "structures" of society, but rather by being acted upon by discourses in the current society that are constantly shifting and changing—therefore, individual identity is constantly shifting as well. It implies that we don't *find* ourselves and we don't *create* ourselves, but rather we act, react, and interact with/in the discourses in which we are currently situated.

(Personal notes, August 18, 1994)

There's many, many, many different ways of bringing feminism into teaching and . . . the person's politics are going to make it different, the situations are going to make it different, and the receivers [are going to make it different]. . . . It's always going to be very, very complicated.

(Julie)

These words described my developing understandings about the meanings and implications of situatedness in discourse and identity creation. Through poststructural lenses, a subject neither creates her social environment nor is created by it. Rather, the interaction and fluid interchange of environmental factors and personal philosophies continually shape and inform each other, often in complicated ways. In an effort to discuss the ways in which social contexts are perceived within teaching environments, I analyze here how various factors have informed and shaped feminist teaching practice and discourse. I consider how social forces, in the constructions of teachers' identities, of students as classroom participants, and of institutional structures and expectations, interacted to continually reshape the enactments of feminist teaching.

In this part of the analysis I have several intentions. To begin, understandings of many contexts created in feminist classrooms can provide useful analyses and tools for considering various implications of these contexts. As Susan Heald (1989) suggested, "[Feminist pedagogical] literature has tended to ignore the various contexts in which we teach, leading to a further marginalization of many people and many issues" (p. 22). Further, Magda Gere Lewis (1993) emphasized that "as feminist teachers we need to be clear not only about the political goals toward which we strive, but as well about the social context within which we wish our students to join us in the struggle" (p. 48). While there have been several analyses of feminist teaching that implicitly address teachers' contextually embedded experiences, a contribution of this section is that it focuses explicitly on the multiple factors that affect and construct feminist teaching practice within those contexts. I believe an analysis of this type is continually needed to consider changing environmental factors at play.

Jennifer Gore (1993) suggested that feminist pedagogies are responsive to the contexts in which they are situated. Yet what are these contexts and how are they recognized, produced, reproduced, and, if so desired, resisted? The answers to these questions remain elusive because of the uniqueness and multiplicity of contexts in which feminist educational experiences are situated. As Kathleen Weiler (1988) suggested,

> Students, like teachers, are historically situated beings, whose complex subjectivities are socially defined and at the same time are internalized and lived. Both students and teachers have experienced and participated in relationships of domination, submission, oppression, and privilege which have helped to shape who they are and how they interpret the world. This recognition of students and teachers as historically situated subjects with conflicting gender, race, and class interests is vital to understanding the possibilities and limits of the classroom. (pp. 124–125)

Teaching and learning experiences are uniquely situated, both a product of and producing intricately complex environments.

What, then, is the use of an analysis such as this if every context is so different that none can be generalized? I do not intend to suggest that factors proposed here as largely shaping practices and discourses available to teachers with whom I spoke can be broadly applied to all feminist teaching. Indeed, there were both similarities and differences among the practices and discourses that these teachers enacted. In this work, I provide examples of the various ways that teachers interpreted and understood certain topics, areas, or influences. In doing so, I hope to provide opportunities for a heightened awareness of the ways in which teachers with feminist understandings have interacted with and experienced the environments in which they worked.

Through the general framework for the chapters in this section, I attempt to both interpret and problematize the existence of multiple factors that construct feminist teaching practice. In this research, I learned that the factors at play in the creation of feminist teaching practices were overlapping, often contradictory, and fluctuating. Here, I divide them into three areas. In chapter 2, I discuss how teachers' personal identities and identity constructions affected their own practices. Throughout, I explore multiple backgrounds and belief systems that informed their work. In chapter 3, I turn to ways in which interactions between students and teachers affected what teachers felt was available to them as feminist teaching practice or discourse. Finally, in chapter 4, I turn to multiple institutional structures that served to shape teachers' enactments of feminist teaching.

CHAPTER 2

Multiplicity in Action:
Working Through Identities

All of the voices or purposes that are our minds must be heard in order for us to achieve not an identity but a more communicative form of life— the possibility of conversational reconciling, both in ourselves and with others.

(Young-Bruehl, 1988, p. 21)

Educators and feminists have identities far beyond those relating specifically to these two labels or constructs. When they participate in higher education classrooms, their identities are layered and integrated in a complex series of negotiations and struggles. These multiple identities are not left at the door when teachers define and take on professional roles in classrooms. Rather, they inform teaching discourse and practice in multiple and intricate ways. As Gloria (25 January) told the class early in the semester, "When you walk into the classroom, you've got to realize you're not just a teacher, but also a person." And Sue Middleton (1995) suggested:

> Rather than presenting theories as a flat, or two-dimensional, map, we can study the ways in which—as teachers, as students, as social researchers and writers—we are positioned "inside" the social and educational phenomena which are the objects of our inquiries. (p. 95)

In this chapter, I look for ways in which teachers' multiple selves or identities found expression in their practices. In doing so, I address the question, How do teachers' multiple identities affect their constructions of what is available in feminist teaching practice and discourse?

Many scholars and educators have considered ways in which teachers' multiple identities have influenced teaching practice (Frye, 1992b; Maher & Tetreault, 1994; Middleton, 1993; Rakow, 1992; Rockhill, 1993;

27

Weiler, 1988; Young-Bruehl, 1988). The themes in their work can be generally placed into two groups. The first grouping, feminist identity, is explored in literature that has suggested that a feminist in a classroom has various experiences that are shaped, at least in part, by her identity as a feminist (Middleton, 1995; Weiler, 1988). The second, which I am terming *political/cultural identities*, centers around identity characteristics such as race, gender, class, and sexuality. Scholars have pointed out that one's background and current statuses in relation to these categories affected the ways in which they were able to construct their classroom practices in terms of communication and relations between class participants (Jipson, 1995; Lewis, 1990; Rockhill, 1993; Weiler, 1988).

In this work, I examine the feminist and political identities of the teachers with whom I spoke, emphasizing throughout ways in which these multiple identities shaped their teaching practices. I explore the relationship between these identities and classroom power and authority, an example that teachers brought up repeatedly in our discussions. Further, I discuss how teachers' identities have been used as teaching tools, and, finally, how those multiple and ever changing identities serve to shape the practices and available discourses in feminist teaching.

IDENTITY CONSTRUCTION IN FEMINIST TEACHING

Feminist teachers, if they are to work to create a counter-hegemonic teaching, must be conscious of their own gendered, classed, and raced subjectivities as they confirm or challenge the lived experiences of their students. This does not mean avoiding or denying conflict, but legitimating this polyphony of voices and making both our oppression and our power conscious in the discourse of the classroom.

(Weiler, 1988, p. 145)

Identity constructions and perceptions influence the range of options and understandings from which teachers and students are able to choose in developing classroom discourses. For my research, I focus on three main themes which heavily influenced and were influenced by identity constructions of the teachers within the feminist classrooms that I studied. First, I examine teachers' self-presentations in terms of their feminist or political/cultural stances. Second, I discuss how both students and teachers related identity constructions to classroom authority. I look at how this relationship between identity and authority was created, understood, challenged, and problematized through classroom dialogue and activities. Third, I consider how teachers used examinations of their identities and identity constructions as educational tools for understanding and critiquing assumed or constructed identities in other forms of social interaction.

Feminist Identity

> There was no split between my personal and my intellectual dilemmas. I lived my feminism. I was inside my own questions and methods, positioned with the object and the process of my inquiries.
>
> (Middleton, 1993, p. 65)

Crafting a political identity while playing a teaching role is difficult in a society and a university environment that have traditionally valued "objective" and "apolitical" knowledge. When one is an assumed leader of a classroom, making explicit one's political identity can be a decision that will greatly affect the dynamics of the class. Additionally, when that political identity is termed *feminist*, an additional set of resistances and questions must be considered. In this section, I discuss how the teachers with whom I spoke sought, with their students, to negotiate their constructions of themselves and their identities as political beings within and outside classroom walls.

Several feminist teachers in this study made their feminism explicit within the classroom. They often chose to do so because they believed that their students were looking for feminist role models or "styles" that they could learn from and potentially emulate. Rosa commented:

> I often think that our students are looking for intellectual models. But I also think that they're looking for personal models. They . . . want someone—a woman preferably, many of them—with whom they can identify. They can say, "This is somebody that I want to be like." And they also want to find thinkers that they want to be like.

Several teachers commented that they believed it was appropriate and useful to their students to identify themselves as feminists both in their teaching and in other work that they did. In terms of students' openness to these teachings, Brianne commented, "One of the nice things about teaching with *feminist* in the title of the course [would have been that] I would have felt no hesitance about positioning myself politically." These classes and situations, however, were largely dependent on the course content and the political leanings of students who chose to enroll.

Other teachers discussed not labeling themselves as feminists until students pressed them to assume such a label. Often, students labeled these teachers as feminist before the class even began. As Rosa described it,

> Sometimes you're marked as a feminist even before you declare yourself one. And I think in certain situations . . . just the way you live your life, the way you conduct yourself, the way you talk about yourself, your self-presentation, gets you labeled as something before you might even say, "Oh, this is what I choose for myself." . . . You're asking different questions. You're raising different points.

Some described the experience of not identifying as explicitly feminist or feminist in a certain way until students questioned them.

In one case, Andrea reflected on why she hadn't explicitly identified herself as a feminist to students in her class. She described to me that she doesn't think she consciously chooses or thinks about feminist teaching because it's so deeply ingrained in her. She said further that being a feminist is deeply ingrained as well. Because it was such an integral and assumed part of who Andrea was, she didn't feel it necessary to discuss her feminism in her teaching.

In a few cases, teachers claimed the term feminist, but were hesitant to identify as feminist teachers because of their unfamiliarity with literature in the area or because of their unwillingness to classify themselves in one way to the exclusion of others. They established that their identities were multiple, shifting, and situation specific.

In the process of deciding how, when, and whether they would make their feminism explicit in the classroom, teachers considered that students would not always share their commitments. They also questioned how their spectrum of political beliefs affected their interactions with students and their creation of feminist teaching practices. As Chris told her class,

> I'm a feminist and there are varieties of feminism. And I'm certainly not a radical feminist by far. And some of you will probably find me too radical and some of you will find me not radical enough, but that's just who I am.

This identification of oneself as feminist is not necessarily done in a way to try to get students to embrace feminist ideals. In one case, Julie said that she wanted students to learn about her political commitments from her, rather than from another source. Whether providing feminist role models, teaching feminist skills, or merely making explicit a struggle for one's own feminist identification, many teachers with whom I spoke suggested that constructing feminist identities in their classrooms affected the teaching and learning that took place.

Political/Cultural Identity

> We are not solitary when we think; we are full of voices.
>   (Young-Bruehl, 1988, p. 17)

Although feminism could be considered a part of one's cultural identity, I turn here more specifically to culture in terms of one's political identification as related to race, gender, class, sexuality, age, or intersections of these identity components. I discuss teachers' understandings of their own cultural identities and how they affected teaching practices.

Teachers' cultural identities could not be separated from their classroom interactions. As such, several teachers talked about the inevitability of their cultural identities entering into classroom discourses. Kathy commented:

> My own identity was sculpted very clearly. . . . There was just no way that I couldn't come in and say: "This is where I am socially. This is why I'm concerned about these issues. Not because of being politically correct right now. But because this is who I am. And all I'm asking you to do is sort of situate yourself and find out who and what you are as related to this course."

Kathy wanted not only her identity, but also the identities of students, to become part of classroom discourses and meaning-making.

In several cases, teachers' understandings of their own ethnic identities influenced their classroom and teaching presentations. Deborah talked about her experiences in this way:

> As a teacher standing in the front of the class . . . of course I realize I'm very much on display. I'm extremely and always conscious of this and this consciousness affects my physical presentation. I'm first of all conscious of being a [woman of color][1] in a largely Caucasian place. I dress conventionally to counteract the strangeness that I expect others are experiencing as they look at me.

And Mary Louise considered the significant influence that her identity had on the content of the courses she teaches as well as on the underlying philosophies that guide her research, teaching, and service.

> I'm a [woman of color], I'm second generation, and so it's personal as well as theoretical. I try with all the material I read to ask questions that focus on who makes the choices in society and the outcomes for different people of various decisions.

Both Mary Louise's and Deborah's presentations and overall belief systems were strongly influenced by the ways in which they identified with their ethnic heritages. They attempted to construct their identities based partly on the presumed implications of those constructions for others both inside and outside of the classroom and the academic institution. Their actions were shaped by the social discourses regarding race that they had both experienced and, in some ways, come to expect through interactions with others.

One teacher talked about her difficulty in bringing in certain course material because of her multiple identity positions. Cheryl described her beliefs:

> I just always try to teach diverse works in terms of . . . talking about women of color, lesbian women . . . but also trying to talk about the texts as a middle-class, straight, White woman. It's not a solely objective text or one that speaks for most women. I try to talk about how race, class, and gender influence that. With the students, it's weird teaching books by women of color—me as a White woman to [many] White students and one African American or [many] White students, 3 Asians, 3 Latinas, and 3 African Americans.

Both her own and students' identity positions affected Cheryl's examinations of her classroom context and strategies that she felt were available and beneficial for developing a classroom discourse.

Gloria emphasized that the intersections between her various identities, rather than any singular aspect, most significantly influenced her decisions about teaching. She described her teaching as multicultural and stated: "I think that if anybody embodies the sort of intersection of multiculturalism, it's women of color with a working-class background. So there's race, class, and gender right there."

IDENTITY AND AUTHORITY

To what extent are our choices shaping who [students] are? To what extent are they shaping who we are?

(Ruth)

The construction of one's identity is closely related to authority in the classroom. Feminist educational literature has emphasized sharing power with or empowering students in an effort to more evenly distribute classroom authority and to diminish potentially negative effects of traditional classroom hierarchies (Bennett, 1991; Dewar, 1991; Luke & Gore, 1992b). Relatedly, some literature has suggested that teachers' and institutions' power must be recognized in order to make explicit power relations that will inevitably exist in these educational situations (Gore, 1993). Yet poststructural thought has insisted that power relations are fluid and identity related. Therefore, the presupposition of uncritical "empowerment" *by* teachers *for* students becomes problematic. Learning to negotiate teachers' authority in higher education feminist classrooms related strongly to identity constructions. In some cases, teachers' identities were constructed in ways that helped establish classroom authority. Among the teachers with whom I spoke, authority was closely linked to appearance or style of presentation, professional background and age, institutional affiliation, and other cultural identity positions.

Several teachers said that they consciously constructed their appearance and style of presentation to help establish and maintain their authority. Deborah talked about her beliefs:

> I realize that power can reside in appearance and clothing. Wearing a jacket makes a difference and gives me authority. Wearing high heels gives me height. . . . If you are a professor, you have to look like a professor. And you can't look like a professor unless you dress like one. So there's a little of that, you know. I'm sort of on this generational bridge trying to adapt and yet feeling that I'm not going to look the part if I don't dress the part. People won't take me seriously. If I go to meetings with deans and other chairs, then I have to dress up more. When I don't teach, I dress down.

Julie's statement supported that view, but added that she at times felt she was compromising—perhaps to the point of "selling out." In her words,

It's real fun for me to look at the many different ways I bring who I am. I mean, literally changing clothes. That's an interesting one. I used to . . . feel I didn't have to dress up for women's studies students. Now, I'm realizing more and more that how I dress is important to women's studies students. . . . It's fascinating for me to watch all those different layers and figure out who I want to be. I constantly struggle with which things are selling out and which are things that I'm willing to do in order *to have people listen*. And I come down on real different sides on different issues.

In order to gain authority in the form of the attention of others to her perspectives, Julie walked a fine line between compromise and selling out.

Other teachers talked about the ways in which they attempted to revise or construct their physical images and identities to elicit certain responses, often in the form of authority, from students. In halting and hesitant speech, Cheryl presented clearly her reasons for and struggles with these concessions:

When I started teaching this class [another teacher] said: ''Go in heavy on authority. Dress up. And just have an authority. You can always relax after that. But you're young and they are going to feel that they don't have to respect you. Or some of them.'' And in many ways I've done that. I dress up more when I'm teaching, I wear makeup when I'm teaching, which I don't when I'm not; but I also question that as well. . . . I have a sense that if I make more visual concessions, then I can say more radical things without getting dismissed. . . . If I am, in my appearance, to a certain extent conceding to ''proper'' professional appearance, then I can say more controversial or challenging types of things without having them think she's one of those radical, hairy-legged, etc. . . . And at the same time I don't want that to be true.

For the teachers with whom I spoke, appearance and choice of dress affected their ability to establish the kinds of authority that they desired within their classrooms. When and how to compromise, though, were decisions not easily made.

Age and experience or professional background also helped teachers establish their desired classroom authority. Several felt confident that students knew their ages and professional backgrounds well enough that they were willing to grant them a measure of authority based on those experiences. Chris talked about her understandings of this occurrence:

> I think students at a lot of universities are very savvy—my name is known. Students talk about me as faculty. There is a lot of word of mouth about courses so they know I've been around here for a long time. They know [my writing] and all that kind of stuff. . . . [They know] what your status is.

Another teacher was unable to describe exactly why students more easily grant her authority in the classroom, but felt strongly that it had something to do with her experience as a teacher in this academic environment. When asked to comment on her power in the classroom, Eileen said:

> I think that it's complicated by lots of factors. . . . There were kinds of insecurities that were written all over me when I started teaching here. There are kinds of problems that I used to have in the classroom that I never, ever, ever have anymore. I think that particularly they were about young men competing with me for power in the classroom. Nobody does that anymore. . . . I'm no longer perceived as available for that.

Several teachers believed that age and professional experience greatly affected the degree of authority that they were able to expect in the classroom.

Teachers also talked about the ways in which their authority was compromised or challenged because of their own identities or identity constructions. Many of these challenges or compromises were, they believed, closely linked to cultural identity positions—usually relating to gender or race. For example, Sharon felt that her classroom authority was often greatly compromised because of larger social assumptions about and expectations for women. She told me:

> Women stepping into a classroom do not have the same authority in a student's mind that men have. I just believe that deeply—the students are always processing the teachers as female. Frequently this means, depending a little bit on the age, the teacher is processed as mother. Mothers are supposed to give all-forgiving love and not be critical. So frequently, in my women's studies classes, before I hand back papers, I will announce: "I am not your

mother. I am critical of your work and I am doing that because that is my job and because I want to help you grow," etc., etc. The issue of authority is something that all women teachers have to deal with whether they deal with it consciously or not. If you use experience and self-disclosure there is no question that you run the risk of making the class seem less academic, of falling into the trap of functioning psychologically as mother or sister or buddy, depending on your age. Those are difficult lines to cross.

Another teacher agreed with her, and commented on a specific class situation to substantiate her claims. Sarah put it this way:

It's been unusual because this has been the first semester where I've had more men than women in the class. And I had a couple of men who have been like prototypical male conversation style types, jumping all over women's words, not letting them finish. And they do that to me. One man actually did this in class, and I had to make a concerted effort to put on a plow, and when he interrupted me I would just keep going. So I had to change my conversational style to make sure that my words were heard. And it was interesting because I saw other women who do the same thing. And it happened in about 2 weeks where we found that—and people didn't talk to each other—they'd just keep going. Also, I think that these things kind of had a devaluing [effect on] the activities in class. Several people have come to me and said, "He would never do that if you were a male professor." And it's been very frustrating to me to know how to handle this.

Both Sharon and Sarah believed that their efforts to establish certain kinds of authority and adopt certain roles with students were constrained by their identities. Several teachers spoke of their struggles to create a basis for authority when, because of their gender, students were hesitant to grant it.

One teacher strongly questioned the notion that institutional power can be enough to compensate for the lack of power or authority that is ascribed to the female body. She suggested instead that students' understandings of what it means to be gendered often override the presumed authority granted to those in university teaching positions. In Rosa's words,

It's a very Foucauldian notion, that anybody who's a part of the institution speaks for it. But that seems to run counter to many of our students' notions here that women don't, by virtue of their positions as women, by gender, don't have authority. [Students are] not used to seeing women as ultimate authorities. So you've got two contradictory positions. For me, I think gender wins out over the institutional authority. Students tend not to pay as much attention to women as they would to men. And so you're sort of looking at contradictory issues. And I think [students] pick up on those contradictions. I think feminists did themselves a disservice by sort of saying, ''Well, we're going to be here to give over some of this power that the institution has invested in us,'' when in fact, the students' first reaction is not to give women that same kind of investment of power that they might give men. . . . I think that it's very conflicting for students. They see a woman in a position of authority and they don't know whether to react to her as a woman or as an authority figure and they tend to try to figure out which one to appeal to her on. What ends up happening is that the woman is sort of divided. . . . We're constantly working against contradictory expectations from students.

Rosa further discussed the different types of authority and conceptions of empowerment that she tried to establish and instill throughout her classroom interactions. She talked about her understandings of feminist authority:

I think it's much clearer with students if you come in and say: ''Yes, I'm a woman. Yes, I'm part of an institution. But I'm going to combine these two different kinds of authorities.'' And one of the ways that I do it is by appealing to feminist authority and saying: ''There's a certain kind of authority that feminists set up that's different from the authority of just a woman teacher or a male teacher. And that authority is vested in this notion of social justice. [The] agenda I have is trying to advance an ethical position—a position that says we're going to have equal time, but we're not *just* going to have equal time, we're going to try to find some collaborative or collective goal.'' And that is the kind of authority that's not just for the self, but for the collective whole that you're trying to represent as well.

Teachers anticipated and responded to students' expectations of their identities in relation to their ethnicities, appearances, professional backgrounds, ages, and genders. Most often, these teachers attempted to problematize the intersections and interactions between their identities in ways that they hoped would afford them with the opportunities to create an educational environment conducive to a variety of educational and feminist goals. However, their perceptions of their own identities, as well as their understandings of students' perceptions, sometimes resulted in these feminist teachers feeling "different" from the norm and "divided" as persons. As several teachers pointed out, though, many feminist teachers have developed the skill to act as chameleons in educational environments. Their multiple identities, in terms of cultural and political characteristics and beliefs, enabled them to relate to students in an educational sense while simultaneously retaining their feminist commitments.

IDENTITY AS A TEACHING TOOL

> How can we teach for radical change if we don't challenge our students' androcentric readings of literary texts or their classist, sexist, racist, and homophobic discourses as they arise in journals, essays, and class discussion? Does challenging these readings and writings necessarily mean denying student subjectivities? Can there be a truly "safe space," in or out of the classroom? Should there be? Is there in our desire for a safe space also a refusal to recognize that our different locations—as men or women, as Anglos or people of color, as faculty or as graduate students—are and have always been unequal?
>
> (Eichhorn et al., 1992, p. 300)

In these educational environments, several teachers talked about how they worked with students to examine identity constructions and to make explicit assumptions and "commonsense" understandings of how various aspects of one's identities affected educational and social processes. Teachers discussed how they incorporated aspects of their own experiences, which comprised their identities, into the classroom for educational purposes.

In one case, Brianne encouraged students to talk about her role as a teacher and to understand the measures that enabled her to occupy that position or identity. As she said,

> What I'm really interested in is sort of a clarity about what is going on institutionally as a larger context for the classroom and making clear why it is the class is being taught, why it is that I'm teaching the class, how it is that I got there, not hiding [the] means of production of presentation. . . . So a lot of what I'm interested in is

just sort of foregrounding those kinds of institutional operations. Which practically for me has meant saying things like: ''I'm teaching this course because I was available in these ways. Here are the ways in which I was able to honestly convince people I was qualified and here are my weaknesses in being here.''

By doing this, Brianne hoped to make explicit different factors that shaped both her identity as an instrument or member of an institution and possible reasons for the constructed experiences that students may have throughout their educational careers.

Gloria (15 February) asserted to her class that teachers' own experiences and cultures could be used to further the educational discourse as well. As I described in my field notes, she defined culture broadly.

[A student] then asked if she should treat people from different cultures differently in class. Gloria responded that this is often the mistake that is made. She pointed out that each class has a culture of its own and also that the culture of the teacher is important to consider [in determining appropriate pedagogy].

Gloria asserted that each teacher's own experiences and cultural backgrounds, as well as the backgrounds and experiences of students, were important for developing what she termed culturally relevant pedagogy.

Other teachers focused on presenting specific aspects of themselves and making those identity positions available for interrogation in order to ensure that the focus of the course wasn't always centered on positions of dominant groups. In one case, a teacher asked that students be involved in ensuring that their own specific identities did not form an exclusive classroom discourse. Julie explained:

My very first class, I ask the class to help me in that I don't want it to be a White, middle-class, heterosexist, young women's class, and [we talk about] how we're going to work on that together. Usually students have no idea at that stage what I'm talking about. . . . The first few weeks what we have is the men being real aware that for the first time, they're in a classroom where they're not the center of attention. But what has happened often is that the White women get real comfortable being the center of attention. And even though I'm trying to teach against that, clearly because I'm a White person in front, there's a way in which women of color must still feel marginalized. . . . It's real different than if it were a Black woman teaching the class.

Cheryl talked about her efforts to encourage students to complicate frameworks when examining identity constructions and assumptions within classroom analyses. She discussed her strategies:

> What's hardest for me is my perspective—not presuming a "we"— that when we read a book by women of color, we [is] assuming most of you who are White and me who is White. One thing I try to do is play with pronouns, "we, you, they, those of us who." I try to use that one a lot. "Those of us who are White"—so it doesn't seem like I'm assuming everyone in the class is White. And also there is of course difference within Whiteness. What is White? . . . I try to continually complicate the frameworks we're working with—add more and more variables to them.

These teachers recognized the impact that their own identities may have had on classroom discourse and tried to encourage students to look at the ways in which teachers' and students' own identities significantly shaped the educational experiences that they created together.

Whereas several of the teachers I spoke with encouraged students to work on "decentering" themselves and their identities in order to learn that skill and turn attention away from dominant perspectives, some talked about how they carefully centered, or focused on, their own identities as teaching tools to enrich students' educational experiences. Vicki described her use of her own experience:

> I very often use aspects of personal experience to bring it to life, to bring the sense of struggle to life for students now, who just grow up with all this stuff on a platter in front of them. . . . I think particularly graduate students very often tend to think of feminist inquiry as very academic. Many of them, in fact, come to it only through an academic groove. They don't come to it through any kind of personal activism, anything they did as undergraduates except course work. It is a set of ideas, [they find it] exciting, but that is the main thing. So frequently I like to bring sharply to their awareness the relationship of feminism in the academy and feminism as an outsider.

In this case, Vicki drew on her experience as an activist outside of the academy to educate students about another, "nonacademic" type of feminist thought and action. At the same time, she problematized this sharing of her own experience when she provided the following example:

> To use disclosure on the part of the teacher is a way to get students to understand the connection between the ideas we study and lived lives. I stress that I did that with a very careful sense of control because I think that can become very narcissistic. Another danger is that any experience that I personally experienced is reproduced by other women in the class or it obscures cultural, racial, religious, [and] sexual differences among women.

Teachers' identities and the experiences that shaped those identities can be used in various ways as teaching tools both to make explicit power relations within certain socially constructed identities and to teach students different perspectives based on events or situations that class participants had not experienced.

TROUBLING IDENTITIES IN FEMINIST DISCOURSE

> Private identity is an oxymoron. Identity is public; it is how one is known. Secret identity, by contrast, is entirely possible. It is not a reflection of inward realities, but of outward realities. Secret identity is a stratagem for survival, the characteristic improvisation of a minority in danger.
>
> (Wieseltier, 1994, p. 26)

> Woven through our theoretical deliberations, our struggles with feminist and sociological theories in education and other sites, are reflections on the everyday practicalities of our experience—as teachers and workers; as researchers; as participants in institutional reorganization and wider political upheaval during times of economic crisis and administrative restructuring; as women whose maternal and civic responsibilities come into conflict with the demands of our professional and political lives.
>
> (Middleton, 1995, p. 99)

These teachers discussed their struggles with their own identity constructions as participants in a feminist teaching discourse in higher education classrooms. They also discussed how they attempted to use and analyze those constructions in their classrooms as educational tools for learning. A feminist poststructural analysis can help us understand these teachers and the struggles that they encountered as they negotiated fluctuating identities and the related "status" or authority that often correlated with those identities.

Much feminist literature has emphasized the need for constant examination of teachers' identities in the shaping of classroom discourses. As Jeanne Brady Giroux (1989) stated, "Teachers also need to be conscious of their own voices so that they can understand how their own values and experiences work to produce, legitimate, and structure how they respond to the various voices that make up their classroom" (p. 9). Kathleen Rockhill (1993) stressed this point when she said:

> The power we confront is not some alien enemy but ourselves, the ways we have learned to be as feminized objects, our life as we have understood it, including the hope for safety and salvation through romance, the home, and the family. (p. 357)

Rockhill's words further Giroux's analysis by suggesting that being conscious is never entirely possible. Being fully aware is perhaps a worthwhile, yet unattainable, goal. Identities affect feminist teaching discourses and practices in ways that we will perhaps never know. Therefore, with Peter McLaren and Colin Lankshear (1993), I believe that

> we must abandon the outmoded and dangerous idea that we possess as social agents a timeless essence or a consciousness that places us beyond historical and political practices. Rather, we should understand our "working identities" as an effect of such practices. (p. 386)

I understand this, as applied here, to mean that teachers take part in constructing their own identities, but others take part as well as they bring socially constructed expectations and assumptions about a feminist teacher's multiple identities into classroom discourses. Therefore, these identities are always fluctuating and contextually bound.

Power relations were not static in these classrooms. Students and teachers had power in different ways based on their multiple identities—all of which were tentative and fluid. Identity, then, is a term that is most useful when broadly defined and seen as perhaps not all-encompassing. The "creation" of identity is impossible, as there exists no time when a totally new and unchanging being enters a discourse. I cannot distinguish such a point in this research. Rather, the concept of identities is, for me, like viewing a borderless map. Many of the landmarks have posted names; indeed, I have lived in places called *White* and *Woman*. Once a location, an identity, is a part of me, I cannot disown it. Yet it need not own me. Rather, I can visit, through careful listening and interaction, other locations whose characteristics and opportunities provide lessons and insights as well. While some people travel more frequently and enthusiastically than others, this process of traveling is endless. As Taunya Lovell Banks (1997) wrote, "My life stories influence my perspective, a perspective unable to function within a single paradigm because I am too many things at one time" (p. 99). Our identities are multiple yet enmeshed with each other in a chaotic balance of life choices and struggles for self.

Relatedly, power and authority were not ultimately and timelessly manifested in the institutionally sanctioned position of *teacher*. Rather, social factors worked to distribute authority to a variety of positions and create assumptions about various identities held by participants in these classrooms. Power relations within feminist classrooms can perhaps be best understood by examining the many sources, patterns, locations, and exceptions that are present within social relationships. The intersections of multiple identities both within and among classroom participants often led to disruptions or gaps in constructed understandings, and subsequently to more fluid and fluctuating relationships within feminist teaching practices and discourses.

Feminist teachers with whom I spoke were keenly aware of the gaps, ruptures, and contradictions that existed in their embodiment of feminist teaching discourse. Teachers realized that as radical individuals within environments not traditionally defined in terms of radical politics (Kerr, 1995), they were considered obvious, "abnormal" (Wasser & Bresler, 1996), and divided. These teachers were in some ways different and sought to either call attention to or lessen the effects of that difference depending on reactions that they anticipated from others. Their struggles within those multiple and sometimes conflicting identities called for continuous reevaluation of what it meant to be both feminists and teachers. The strategies and outcomes of these struggles, I learned, took many forms.

Students and teachers construct classrooms in which they work, learn, and teach with and for each other. While their characteristics, practices, attitudes, and philosophies are not the only factors shaping this environment, students and teachers are actors and enactors simultaneously and fluidly in their classroom practices. Although the educational experiences presented here are not uniform, they nevertheless lead us to different understandings of dynamics within feminist classrooms. They also provide clues for the ways in which identity constructions can both foster and stifle educational efforts. Teachers can utilize constructions of identity and difference as classroom content to problematize assumptions and expectations based on fixed understandings of group identity. They can use their own identities and experiences to demonstrate political options and choices. And teachers can help students begin to see the value and necessity of coming to know and question through an examination of the ways that we construct identities—both for ourselves and for others.

CHAPTER 3

Unsettling Roles: Teacher and Student Interactions

What is required . . . is attention to open-ended and specific pedagogies, sensitive to context and difference, addressed to the social position of any learning group and the positions of the individuals within it.

(Lusted, 1986, p. 10)

There are ways in which teaching is a little like parenting, that is you set something in motion but you simply can't control it. And that is, of course, exciting.

(Vicki)

It seems that nearly all analyses of feminist teaching or feminist classrooms recognize multiple relations and interactions among teachers and students. Because of the often relational methods associated with feminist work, students are certainly one of the main influences on practices perceived as available within feminist teaching discourse. Some authors have concentrated on what feminist education or feminist teachers should give or provide to students (J. Giroux, 1989; Luke, 1992). Others have discussed the ways in which student knowledges and experiences are brought into classroom practices (Lee, 1994; Lewis, 1990; Maher, 1985). Still others have concentrated on the numerous forms of student resistance that they have witnessed or felt in their teaching efforts (Lewis, 1990; Orner, 1992). Student-teacher relationships have affected teaching practices in many ways.

In this analysis, drawing on feminist poststructuralism led me to look closely at how power relations and negotiations between students and teachers shaped enactments and constructions of feminist teaching. I concentrate here on various ways in which teachers attempted to be responsive to students in learning environments. Because feminist teaching literature generally viewed students as integral to the shaping

of educational environments, teaching practices often incorporated reflection on varying beliefs and abilities of students. Therefore, feminist
teaching practices were largely situation specific.

In this chapter, I supplemented the presentation of teachers' interview data and class observation data with student feedback that I gathered at the end of the two classes that I observed for a semester. I do not
intend students' words to be measures of Mary Louise's and Gloria's
"success" in responding to students. Instead, I see student feedback as
one further source of data to consider when attempting to understand
ways in which student and teacher relationships affected feminist teaching practices and discourses. Approximately half of the students involved in these classes submitted written responses to my request for
any comments they may have had about Mary Louise's and Gloria's
teaching or about their experiences in these two classes. As I planned to
share these comments with Mary Louise and Gloria, I told students that
this was my intent, but that they could remain anonymous if they desired. The student texts that I chose to supplement this chapter largely
pertained to the themes that I generated in relation to feminist teaching's responsiveness to students.

STUDENTS' INFLUENCE ON ENACTMENTS
OF FEMINIST TEACHING

While it may seem self-evident that students are a large part of
any classroom experience, in much feminist teaching practice student
experiences and expectations are *central* to teaching and learning. Feminist teaching practice therefore attempts to incorporate or address the
varying positions of students. In this section, I propose that an integral
part of feminist teaching discourse in this research was a responsiveness
to student experiences in at least two ways. First, feminist teaching
practice shifted the content and expression of that content to better
respond to students' learning positions. These positions were affected
by a multitude of background, cultural, and educational factors. Those
enacting feminist teaching were aware of the fluctuating roles or positions that were available to both teachers and students; as such, they
attempted to address and construct these roles in ways that they
thought would be most helpful for creating a comfortable, yet challenging environment. Second, many enacting feminist teaching cared about
students' experiences both in and out of the classroom, expressing this
in a variety of ways.

Shifting Content and Expression

> The readings you bring to our group and your unassuming pedagogy of
> raising questions from our interactions with the text has been, and still is,
> a transforming experience for me. It's the kind of teaching that brings me
> closer to my vision of teaching.
>
> (Student, Letter to Mary Louise)

In order to incorporate multiple perspectives and experiences of
students in their classes, several teachers in this study attempted to shift
the content and their teaching expression in ways that encouraged and
enabled student learning. Several teachers talked about the difficult but
important task of getting to know students' experiences and expectations with/in classroom environments. Based on this understanding,
some teachers approached class members in challenging ways those
urged them to expand their ways of thinking. For example, Rosa consciously chose to teach about an approach that was contradictory to
those of many other women's studies faculty. Andrea challenged her
students in another way, encouraging them to seek and develop their
own truths about course content rather than "providing" them with the
truth that they have come to expect in formal education. Andrea said:

> There are multiple knowledges out there that sometimes I access,
> sometimes the students access . . . but we don't all believe them
> all in the same way. Sometimes students will ask me "truth" ques-
> tions. We spend a lot of time talking about [that]. . . . They really
> want some truth. They want me to tell them something. And you
> know, I don't, and that totally pisses them off and that's really
> hard for them. I think that has a lot to do with what kind of devel-
> opmental stage that they might be at or how they see the world
> working in their lives.

Finally, at the end of a particularly intense discussion on assessment,
Mary Louise explained her challenging behavior to other class members:

> One of the reasons I spoke from the right or whatever tonight is be-
> cause the tendency when talking about assessment is to come up
> with the solution . . . and I think it's more complicated than that.
> . . . I don't think there's an answer to this—it's an art.

There were many situations in which those enacting feminist teaching acknowledged the locations, positions, and identities of their students and encouraged them, through challenging class material and questioning, to consider the usefulness and potential drawbacks of those positions.

Teachers frequently chose to use a different strategy as well. Depending on the situation, feminist teachers would slightly shift the content they brought to the classroom, or their expression of that content, so that it would be easier for students to understand or relate to it. From my participation in and observations of the first day of Gloria's class (25 January), I believe that she was trying to set the tone of the class for student involvement in the determination of class content. She asked that everyone write for several minutes about either their worst or their best teacher. While she designated who would write on each, students' (and my own) reactions to this exercise indicated that people easily related to either topic. In my field notes, I wrote:

> The experience in this class was powerful. The writing exercise was moving—it really helped me in framing why it was so important to think and talk about teaching. The "good teacher" stories were told with twinkles in the eyes and smiles on the faces of the tellers, usually in a loving poet's language. The "bad teacher" stories were told with grimaces and short, crisp words that seemed to characterize the teachers as much as did [the meanings of the words] themselves. The activities that we did didn't feel like educational activities. I guess I really didn't learn any facts. But I learned a technique and I learned a feeling that made me extremely conducive and open to learning.

The approach that Gloria took to opening that semester engaged students from the very beginning and established that they would contribute to and affect the content and practices of the class.

In many other ways, teachers sought to understand students' needs and expectations for the class and for their educational interactions. I listened as Kathy strongly encouraged her class to be honest and thorough in their evaluation of her, because their evaluations helped her to shape her teaching. I watched as students in several classes regularly interrupted their teachers so that they could be an integral part of framing classroom discussion. And I observed as Sarah, in considering students' lack of response to a question she had posed, asked, "Is [this topic] not worth talking about? That's a possibility."

Julie asserted that another way to make the class material more accessible and responsive to students' expectations was to refrain from assuming that everyone had the same viewpoints or rationale for being involved in the course. She said:

> I was shocked my first semester here. I was shocked and depressed. There's a huge number of people here [for whom] . . . the excitement of learning is not what they're here for. They're here because they need a university degree to get a job. And my challenge is always—can I win them over? But I also have to value that that's a decision—this isn't going to be as important to everybody as it is to me. . . . One of the things that I have to really work hard on in my teaching is just because we eat, sleep, and drink feminism and want it in our teaching, some students just need three . . . credits. What's the big deal? Why is anybody getting all excited about this? They just want to know how to get an A in the course. So real different things happen.

Julie worked hard not to exclude any of the students in her class who chose to enroll for any reason. In her words, "A whole lot of feminist teaching is not excluding anybody."

Other teachers responded to students in continually reactive ways by shaping course material and lecturing topics according to what they perceived students needed or wanted. Andrea talked about the ways in which students shaped—and even inspired—her classroom presentation:

> The students are really important to me, so my lecture styles, the interaction [and] the class is really about them. . . . I structure all the meetings. I know what's important. I lecture on what I think is important. But . . . what the lecture turns out to be is based on them. I mean they might not realize it, but what they say motivates things I say in the front of the room.

An observation of Andrea's class poignantly illustrated both a desire not to exclude students and to respond to what she was perceiving from them in class. In this situation, the content focused on the construction of female sexuality. In an effort to cover text that she thought was important and not exclude anyone or discourage their participation, she told the men in the class, "I'm really sorry, men. This is not a dis on you."

While teachers tried to be responsive to their students in teaching styles and content presentation, they also realized that students' viewpoints, beliefs, and preferred learning styles changed over time and between semesters, as each classroom had its own unique interplay of persons and perspectives. Eileen said that the interactions among class members produced different environments depending on the semester and topic. In her words,

> The first thing is always understanding that what's going to [be] produced is changing. That is part of the sensitivity of who is in this particular group. How did this group of people come together this year in a way that is not like last year? How might, in this setting, this set of people feel empowered by some aspect of their own production?

Further, Andrea asserted:

> Every place or person who is teaching is going to be different. Every class is going to be different. . . . The choices that I make this semester are going to be different, even though the format is the same. The students are going to be different and I'm going to have [different teaching assistants], or choose different readings.

A "reading" of the group of current students, teachers insisted, did not take place only once at the beginning of the semester. Teachers continually tried to discern the degree of comfort and engagability of students throughout the semester. Mary Louise talked about how she stayed aware of the group dynamics in her situation:

> I think what I try to do is feel out the temperature of the group. And as the semester goes on and people are more and more comfortable saying hard things about the readings and to each other about each others' comments, then I try to make the group consider a different dimension of something. I don't believe in levels; I don't think it's bringing the conversation to a higher level—that's not the kind of conversation I would have. Rather, I'm trying to bring out a different dimension of the conversation.

At one point in her reading of the class, Mary Louise sensed that students were not understanding or appreciating the language used in a particular text, and were therefore trying to avoid incorporating it into the discussion. Although she asked that they read the piece and, perhaps, struggle with it, she agreed that it was difficult to read and that it was written in a noninclusive way. Rhetorically addressing the author of this piece, she said, "You're playing a game here with us. And *I'm so smart* is the game."

Gloria talked about how attention to and development of the relationships with and among students in her classrooms fostered a positive classroom environment. In her words,

> This class in many ways is further ahead of many of my classes because the interpersonal relationships seem to be coming together. And I think that is a key ingredient in people's level of satisfaction and they are willing to really say what they believe—that they aren't afraid of the other people.

Teachers' perceptions often served as gauges to help them ascertain when and how challenging topics could be introduced and discussed. This continual awareness of student experiences and expectations resulted in classroom environments that consequently shifted class content and teaching practice to match students' needs and experiences.

Incorporating and Caring about Student Experience

> Gloria's classroom is a haven from the competitive, oppressive world of academia. Every week we gather together to read, write, dialogue, and think. Such a rarity, and luxury, in the research-focused, content-driven world of higher education. Gloria creates an environment where thinking is encouraged and expression of thoughts is valued. . . . This valuing of student voices reflects the importance Gloria places on the knowledge we, as students, possess and the life experiences we have had.
> (Student, Letter to Gloria)

> Can I tell a story? It seems to be the place to tell stories—that people will listen.
> (Student, Mary Louise's class, 14 February)

Feminist teachers sought to incorporate student experience in many ways in their classrooms. As seen above, they attempted to be cognizant of student perspectives and to adapt their teaching to serve purposes related to their students' expectations and needs. Teachers also encouraged students to examine their personal experiences as they related to the content at hand. Further, these teachers paid attention to and solicited feedback from students about their classroom experiences. In other words, how students were experiencing and learning within the teachers' constructed educational environments was deemed as being important to the further development of the course. I focus specifically on knowledge negotiation processes and personal experience in relation to those processes in chapter 6; here I consider my understandings of how an attention to student experiences in a variety of ways related to teachers' expressed "caring" for students.

In many small but seemingly cumulative ways, my observations continually reinforced the idea that the majority of the teachers in my study cared for their students and about their experiences in the classroom. Through encouraging students to introduce themselves and get to know each other, Kathy, Mary Louise, and Gloria tried to build classroom communities in which everyone was a member. Through knowing students' names and recalling their previous comments, even in large classrooms, Andrea and Rosa conveyed that they knew who students were and valued their presence and participation. By asking students to bring in books and to discuss childhood readings, Ruth encouraged students to relate their own experiences to new course content. Further, by inquiring about students' outside lives, many teachers indicated an interest in *persons*, rather than only in *students*.

Mary Louise clearly demonstrated this commitment to incorporating and caring about student experience in the crafting of both classroom content and expression. On a handout that she provided for the class early in the semester (31 January), she wrote, "I hope that the stories of 'others' that you read and write and help others write this semester will become for you . . . places to think about your practices with students." She commented as she handed out readings for students that, "I have to know that you have what you need, or I worry about you." And when pushed to provide clearer boundaries on a particular assignment, she said, "I've talked to a lot of people and people are doing very diverse things. I think you need to do what you need to do."

Oftentimes, a quarter to half of the class was focused on teaching and learning stories that students brought to the group for discussion. These stories quickly became illustrative of the intense struggles that students were experiencing as they thought about and incorporated their educational understandings in other areas of their lives. When a student described a teaching incident, and relayed that he was still "bleeding inside" from it, Mary Louise described a similar incident that she had experienced and, although spending only a brief time on it, related that she empathized with his situation. Throughout the semester, students contributed articles, quotes, readings, videos, announcements, and questions to the classroom discourse that was developing. In each case, Mary Louise provided them with time in class to share what they thought was important enough to bring to the group. She cared about and valued their outside experiences and believed them to be useful to others in the class as well.

Gloria also demonstrated caring about her students and their experiences. The semester began with an exercise in which students' words served as the content for class, and it ended in a similar vein. Additionally, on the front page of her syllabus, she quoted bell hooks: "To teach in a manner that respects and cares for the souls of our students is essential if we are to provide the necessary conditions where learning can most deeply and intimately begin." Finally, throughout the class, she provided many opportunities through diverse classroom activities for students to participate in and engage with the course material. As she reminded students in many different ways, "I want your views."

While most teachers described their use of student experience as a critical analytical piece in educational experiences that they were trying to construct, several acknowledged that this was not always easy to do. In some cases, students were not willing to acknowledge that their experiences could potentially be valuable learning tools. Others were resistant to incorporating their thoughts because this request for disclosure and experience incorporation was not typical in their other educational experiences.

In the two classes that I observed on a regular basis, both Gloria and Mary Louise addressed the issue of disclosing personal experiences explicitly in class. In respecting students' comfort levels in sharing experiential information and simultaneously recognizing its possibilities, both teachers provided classroom options that included the use and analysis of personal experience. They also explicitly stated, however, what they did and did not expect in terms of personal revelation. As Mary Louise was describing an assignment in class, she recounted how she had asked people to do an autobiography in the past, but because it was painful for some, she created another option for people to choose. She also commented that she didn't want anyone to feel that they had to reveal something against their wishes: "I don't think it's our privilege to know everything about everybody. This needs to be a safe place."

Gloria made a similar request that students not disclose information or experiences with which they were uncomfortable. In capital letters on an assignment which had, as an option, the incorporation of personal experience, Gloria wrote, "DO NOT FEEL COMPELLED TO SHARE THINGS ABOUT YOURSELF THAT YOU WOULD RATHER NOT SHARE!" Both of these teachers provided options, so that students could utilize their own experiences as educational tools to the degree that they were comfortable and thought it useful to do so. Gloria and Mary Louise wanted to hear stories and experiences related to students' learning, but they did not want to push students beyond their levels of comfort nor the assignments beyond educational usefulness related to purposes of that particular class or subject area.

As I learned in interviews and observations, these teachers not only cared about the experiences that students brought into the classroom from previous situations, but also about the ways in which students were experiencing current classroom environments that were being constructed. Chris talked about the ways in which she tried to improve students' experiences in her classroom:

> I'm enthusiastic—I try to present [content] in an interesting fashion, and so on. And I am respectful of [students] for what they have to say. I think that if you set that up as a basis, some of the other things aren't as important—if there is basically a good atmosphere and good morale in the classroom. . . . When there is that basic good feeling, that feeling of good relationship between faculty and student, then you can deviate a lot. You can do more lecture and less discussion or more discussion and less lecture—that those things aren't as critical.

Gloria described her thoughts in a slightly different way, noting that classroom experience was important for her as well as for students:

> I try to make us feel like—and I'm stretching the word—family. But there is something that is social, like bringing in food for class members. It's very convenient that we meet over dinner. So there is a rationale for it. But I think when you have those kind of obligations to each other, it tends to bring people together. . . . We're connected to each other. And I've never been happy in a classroom that doesn't have that. It's important.

Through a commitment to each other in terms of class experience, in this case by bringing food for and creating obligations to other class members, Gloria attempted to craft an environment in which students valued their own and others' classroom experiences.

Other teachers talked about how they interacted with students outside the classroom in an effort to make the student-teacher relationship a positive one for learning. Mary Louise discussed how she tried to make students' experiences positive when they were working with her:

> I make a conscious effort to put myself out to people who are in my classes. . . . to say, "You're not just a student in my class, but

you're somebody I appreciate." So if I see them somewhere in the building or in the hall, I might say something personal. Not so much about the class work and such, but to say, "You were so funny the other night, you made me laugh," or "Wasn't it nice when you made somebody feel great?" Because I think when people feel positively, they can learn in a different way. It frees them.

Tonika discussed how the students in her class came to feel comfortable with their classroom experiences as well, and highlighted the ways in which she tried to contribute to their comfort. As she said,

[Students] weren't all that comfortable to begin with. It was also curious to see that by the end of the class, that had completely disappeared. . . . It works. It actually works. It doesn't work because you wish it to work; it works because you sort of watch it and make sure that people are included. And in that class, it's possible to identify somebody who may be having difficulty with something or other and it may be possible to talk to that person, setting up a time to ask, "What's going on here? What's the problem?" So it means working at it and not just thinking that the teacher's job is to prepare for a lecture and walk in and give the lecture. I don't think that that's good teaching.

Tonika, and many others, discussed their efforts to value student experiences, both in terms of educational content and practices, and ways in which they attempted to craft their current environments to demonstrate and implement care for students.

TROUBLING STUDENT RESPONSIVENESS
IN FEMINIST DISCOURSE

The class *is* open to opposing viewpoints and ideas; as Gloria said, she encourages them. However, I rarely heard anyone contradict Gloria or other researchers with ideas similar to hers. I don't know that anyone with a different viewpoint would feel comfortable in her class . . . In many ways, this is a Gloria's disciples class. I'm not sure if that is good or bad— just an observation.

(Student, Gloria's class)

This is supposed to be a world class research institution and I have obligations not only to . . . teachers who are coming in and trying to rethink

what they're going to do tomorrow with . . . their class, and also those
people who are working on master's degrees. I also feel [a] tremendous
obligation to doctoral students who are going to have to go out and com-
pete in the academic marketplace. That's putting it grossly but I'm serious
about that. And we have to provide them with theoretical grounding for
not only the things they write about, but [also for] the actions they're going
to take as academicians. So I'm always wondering, did I do enough?

(Mary Louise, Interview)

Feminist teaching practices and discourses create a variety of ways
in which to respond to students and their expectations of educational
experiences. Not all these teachers thought about or responded to their
students in the same ways. Some felt that students should play a major
role in constructing classroom discourse; others thought that students
should only participate in a relatively circumscribed environment. Additionally, as seen in the student comment above, attempts to create class
comfort may have been successful only for certain students, the "disciples," perhaps, of that teacher or her practices. Students were prepar-
ing for a wide range of future opportunities with a very broad scope of
previous experiences. They therefore had many different characteristics
to which teachers could choose to be "responsive."

What is truly responsive teaching? What happens when students
refuse to play any of those roles that teachers expect of them? What
happens when students do not intend to actively construct a classroom
discourse or participate in prescribed ways by sharing their personal
experiences? How do teachers construct feminist teaching when they
and their students each exist in multiple, seemingly contradictory, contexts? Why do teachers desire to be responsive to students? As Elizabeth
Ellsworth (1993) suggested, teaching to support the diversity that exists
in class participants, what she termed "unassimilated difference," is
indeed a challenge. I will focus more specifically on resistance in chapter
5; here I want to problematize the notion that teachers can ever be
thoroughly responsive to students. I am not certain that we can ever
fully understand what responsiveness means. Rather, mutual yet fluctuating responsiveness and resistance among students and teachers creates a classroom discourse that is shaped by all participants into, as
Gloria suggested, a unique classroom culture.

Jeanne Brady Giroux (1989) described this well when she stated:
"A critical feminist pedagogy does not stop at entitling students to
speak of their own experiences. But neither does it overly privilege voice
so as to substitute critical affirmation for a vague and sloppy relativism"
(p. 9). When applied to the notion of teacher responsiveness to stu-

dents' needs, concerns, desires, or expectations, this statement translates, for me, into a call for negotiations and incorporations of multiple experiences. However, it also calls for the teacher alone to determine what is meant by "a vague and sloppy relativism." The power of responsiveness, in this statement, is in the hands of the teacher. Giroux further pointed out her reasoning for suggesting that power to respond should remain there:

> A critical feminist pedagogy runs the risk of sustaining conscious and subliminal patriarchal behaviors and beliefs that are embedded in ethnic, class, and race realities if students' voices are not critically examined as having specific effects in relations to other human beings. (p. 9)

Feminist poststructuralism urges us to look closely at the assumed and socially constructed boundaries of those who participate in formal and informal educational processes while simultaneously questioning motivations for engaging in those processes.

While problematizing those boundaries and the subsequent categories that they create, feminist poststructuralism nevertheless considers the ways in which these race, class, and gender realities (as well as those of other groups understood to be oppressed) have informed and affected the environments that we are able to expect and create. As multiple identities and desires of teachers and students interact in classroom environments that are already situated in institutions and societies that have understandings and power hierarchies of their own, the negotiation of types of and motivations for responsiveness continues to disquiet feminist teaching discourse.

CHAPTER 4

Mapping the Terrain:
Institutional Barriers, Supports,
and Strategies

Universities are both the site where reactionary and repressive ideologies and practices are entrenched and, at the same time, the site where progressive, transformative possibilities are born.

(Lewis, 1993, p. 145)

Intermingling with each other, feminist teaching discourse and higher education institutions shape each other gradually through sometimes subtle, sometimes harsh interactions. As one of the social forces that affects constructions of and possibilities for feminist teaching, higher education institutions and the structures that support and maintain them often influence possibilities for constructing feminist teaching discourse. Through listening to the voices of research participants, observing their practices, examining related literature, and forming my own understandings, I closely explore in this chapter the many ways that constructions of higher education disrupt, support, and otherwise influence feminist teaching practice. I suggest that there is not a stable or consistent understanding of feminist teaching. Instead, it is constantly shifting and changing based on interactions with its multiple environments and expectations.

As with any work performed within larger institutional or organizational structures, there are certain guidelines and expectations—both implicit and explicit—that affect the ways in which those within those structures operate. While having their own set of unique characteristics, higher education institutions are no exception. Norms and expectations were present in different ways for different people in this research, and the feminist educators with whom I spoke continually renegotiated their roles as teachers within those expectations. As Jennifer Gore (1990) described it, teaching feminism in a classroom remains "an act of pedagogy in an educational institution" (p. 61).

In this chapter, I look at ways in which feminism and higher education disrupted each other, especially as these disruptions affected those using feminist teaching and trying to create feminist learning environments. In each section, I also discuss ways in which feminist teaching discourse utilized and shaped institutional characteristics to better meet the needs of feminist education. Rather than establishing a dichotomy of disruptions and support by these conceptualizations, I urge the reader to see this discussion as representing a snapshot of interactions that are fluid and mutually shaping and whose boundaries are not altogether clear.

SYSTEMIC STRUCTURES

Systemic structures as defined here refer to the various institutionally created arrangements that shape the practices of those who participate in that system. Systems of higher education have long established and retained their norms of practice. These norms of understanding and practice continually reinstate systems of propriety to which those enacting feminist educational discourse are often held accountable.

Oftentimes, feminist teachers operating within higher education systems must contend with a variety of barriers and constraints to their practices (Frye, 1980; Kolodny, 1988). As Jennifer Gore (1993) contended, feminist teachers in the academy are in difficult positions because they are working in social institutions, the premises of which they are often seeking to change. This change is made increasingly difficult both because of the training that feminist teachers have received, and because of the conforming nature of higher education institutions. As Vivian Makosky and Michele Paludi (1990) asserted,

> The stereotype is of the academy as a place where new ideas, approaches, and views are welcome. Although educational institutions may be more liberal than society at large, the fact remains that they are strong pressed toward conformity to the status quo operating in the academy. (p. 8)

The systemic structures perceived by teachers with whom I spoke often shaped their implementation of feminist principles in their classroom practices.

Many teachers expressed their discomfort with practices that they were able to construct within their current institutional—and subse-

quent classroom—structures. Brianne expressed her questionings about
the institutional and academic processes that affected teaching:

> I think one of the big problems in trying to rethink how higher edu-
> cation can happen is that . . . one has to plan things in this struc-
> tured way. The idea that the syllabus happens before you meet the
> students is not actually as obvious as it seems. I can't imagine
> when I will get a chance to teach a course that I don't have to know
> what I'm doing 3 months in advance. But on some level that's one
> of the most basic things that seems wrong to me, or not natural to
> me, at least. The idea to be able to become the teacher that the class
> needs, or the class to become the course that the students need,
> there is not a lot of room for that just in the tradition of college
> teaching.

Other teachers considered traditional structures of college teaching to
work against feminist practices in teaching as well. Andrea said the
following:

> The structure itself, the lecture/[teaching assistant] structure isn't
> feminist. That just seems way too black and white but it's so alienat-
> ing for a student to sit in a [large][1] lecture and take notes for 50 min-
> utes. So that doesn't really build a sort of stronger sense of self or
> care. . . . If I had a [midsized] class and I met with them once a
> week or three times a week for 50 minutes, there would be some
> kind of rapport.

Nearly all of the teachers who were involved with the structure that
mandated a lecture given by the instructor and then separate interactions with teaching assistants commented similarly on the lack of con-
tact that they had with their students and the subsequent lack of rapport
they developed. Tonika said of her larger class:

> I don't get to know the students, or very many of the students,
> very well because [in] those larger classes . . . more students meet
> as small sections with [teaching assistants]. So I never see those stu-
> dents unless they have complaints against the [teaching assis-
> tants]—that's the only time they ever come to see me. I don't grade
> their papers. I don't get to know them.

And in Ruth's class, I observed that the size of the room and the type of
equipment used dictated a certain approach. In my field notes, I wrote:

The class was definitely focused around Ruth. I don't know that there was any way to avoid this, as she had the microphone in a class where it was necessary to use it. Very infrequently did students respond to each other without Ruth's response in between. Students raised their hands and Ruth called on them.

And Vicki said that although her class was one in which personal experience was encouraged and contributed to class discussions, there was very little self-disclosure on the part of the students in her larger classes.

Perhaps the most frequently mentioned problem that teachers discussed in terms of the current university and classroom structure was the size of the classes that they were expected to teach. Teachers told me, closely intertwining what they said with their comments on structure, that having large classes substantially changed the educational experiences that they were able to craft with their students. Julie talked about her classes and the effect that the size had on those experiences:

> You can do so much more in a smaller class. . . . I'd get to know what their lives were, and so then you can really move much more in dangerous territory. But with the large class, you had no idea and it could just totally get out of hand. So you have to be much more cautious in that situation.

Tonika added:

> If you have a manageable group of students together for 3 hours or even for an hour and a half, sometimes . . . you can still create . . . a kind of atmosphere in which you as teacher, you reach beyond simply giving them something intellectual and express your own humanity and help them to express theirs in ways that are not written in the textbooks.

She expressed that this was extremely difficult for her to do with the larger classes she teaches.

Although this was not a common theme, Julie discussed the benefits of teaching in a class environment with many students. While acknowledging the drawbacks to this type of arrangement, she asserted:

> Part of the payoff for me in having to teach these [large] classes I have . . . is so many more people get exposed to this material than normally would if I would have small classes . . . like I would love

to. So the payoff is many, many people who otherwise would
never take it, get it.

In Julie's mind, systemic structures can both support and constrain
one's educational practice, often simultaneously.

What values does this structure of higher education support? As
seen by the preceding comments, feminist values and principles of interaction and mutually decided direction were limited by the size and
structures of the classes that institutional structures established.
Whereas these institutional structures may have supported "efficiency"
goals of the institution, the production model of education seemed to
contradict some goals of feminist classrooms. For example, while several
teachers discussed the benefit of constructing knowledge by exploring
students' experiences, they found this difficult to do in large classrooms. Many teachers recognized that decisions about systemic structures indeed represented statements of values and, subsequently, the
power needed to assert those values throughout the institution.

Several teachers talked about their understandings that the institution did not support or value classroom teaching. Gloria (12 April) described it to students in class: "Even in the academy, teaching is the
lowest of all the things that we do. . . . So the reward structure we're in
says that teaching isn't valued, and therefore it's not closely monitored." Gloria added that students, who have the lowest status in this
institution, are the ones who judge her. One student in Gloria's class
(12 April) described how much she appreciated the environment in the
department in which Gloria and Mary Louise taught: "It's so nice to be
in [this department] because people know how to teach. . . . This is a
place where you can be assured that you're not stupid. Your voice will
be heard. There's possibility here." Yet Gloria said that even in her
department, professors don't necessarily observe or discuss each other's teaching.

Several teachers attempted to examine possibilities and limitations
of institutional expectations of power within other social systems that
retain their own assumptions and understandings of appropriate stan-
dards for interaction. Eileen talked about how she used her own experiences within institutional environments to reshape power dynamics in
her classroom:

One of the things that I think about as teaching as a feminist is for
me, as a woman, a lot of institutional power has been very insidi-
ous in that you simply don't know what the rules are, and they're
not laid out. They're passed on from mouth to mouth. . . . If I

want to make my classroom feel like a less threatening place for women or for people of color who don't fall into getting or being on the inside track in information sharing, what I do is I make the information real blatant. . . . I go out of my way to try to figure out for myself, what are the subtle rules that I operate by? And [I try to] make them clear and up-front, so people have in front of them sort of all the information that I can possibly foreground for them, and then they can operate in that. They can operate within that. But in a way it is a much more bureaucratic and rigid classroom, rather than a more free-flowing and fluid classroom. So the argument that I'm making is that in that fluidity, in that laissez-faire, . . . often kinds of pressure have been perpetuated just by default. If you give everybody all the rules, even if they are obvious rules, again up front, you sort of level the field somewhat. We say, ''In this room, we've all got this set of rules together.''

Eileen attempted to expose and make clear institutional norms and expectations so that she could ''level the field'' and provide persons with a variety of experiences and cultures with as equal an opportunity as possible to succeed in her class.

Most teachers with whom I spoke understood feminist approaches to be those that required challenging institutional norms, structures, and expectations. Vicki talked about it in this way: ''The program itself has argued quite self-consciously that the field of women's studies is not just the study of women, it is the study of women from an oppositional or feminist point of view.'' Teachers continued to probe and test their university environments in their efforts to understand how they could reconcile or disrupt university expectations with their conceptions of useful educational experiences through the lenses available in feminist teaching discourse.

A final structure mitigating feminist teaching practice that I discuss here is that of the tenure process. A primary factor that these educators considered when they were constructing classroom experiences and teaching strategies was not only where students were in educational processes, but also where they themselves were in their tenure process.

One teacher talked about her view that tenure provides professors with the ability to do work that they wanted to do on their own time line. Eileen put it this way:

Once you have tenure, what is the institution going to do to you? And even for that matter, once you are out of school, nobody is giving you a deadline. Nobody is saying, ''Think about this set of

things." And nobody is coming back and saying, "Excuse me, I'm
sorry, but I care that you failed to produce a book this year." . . .
After you leave school, nobody looks at your work that carefully
ever, ever again.

She believed that once tenure is achieved, professors were relatively
free from institutional pressure to do certain types of teaching and research.

Mary Louise told me about her experiences with teaching after she
had successfully achieved tenure:

All the boulders I've been carrying around on my shoulders or in
my body—all the tension that I don't even think I knew was there.
Some of it was subtle, some of it was less subtle. It's gone. It's like
it washed away, or it dropped away, it dropped away. So I hadn't
thought about it in relation to my teaching, but I'm wondering if
it's a combination of things that made [positive class interactions]
come faster this time or it seemed so to me.

Further, she stated:

I think that the burden of my anxiety about my tenure is gone. And
I am so much more relaxed about myself and who I am. Now earlier in the semester than ever before because the tenure process is
over. I just feel more comfortable in class.

The tenure process affected the degree to which some teachers felt comfortable doing their work—both in terms of research and teaching.

ROLE EXPECTATIONS

Within systemic structures are expectations for behavior on the part
of the system's participants. In higher education generally, behavior on
the part of professors or instructors is measured and expected in relation
to a three-pronged ideal of research, teaching, and service. In my study,
those engaging within feminist teaching often struggled with what they
perceived to be expected of them by the higher education institution
and feminist discourses in which they took part.

To illustrate, teachers often discussed their beliefs that despite attempts to eradicate power from the teaching roles that they assumed,

there was no way to avoid the institutionally sanctioned power that they held by virtue of their positions. Tonika put it like this:

> There isn't such a thing as nonhierarchical. That's a term that feminists sort of got into trouble with, got caught on for a long time—that you could create a nonhierarchical classroom for instance where the teacher and the student are equals in the classroom. I don't believe that, and I don't believe that because I never ask my students with any seriousness, "What grade should I give you for this course?" . . . Because even if the teacher were to say to the students, "Well, each of you give yourselves the grade you think you deserve this semester and I will just simply take it like that and put it through like that," the fact is that it is within the teacher's power to say that. . . . So on the basis of the fact that the bottom line for any course is the grade that the student gets—I mean, that's the common denominator—every student who takes the course gets a grade in the course. The grade is always given by the teacher. That in itself, if nothing else, creates a power dynamic in the classroom.

Jasmine discussed how this expectation of authority and power played out in terms of evaluation in her classroom:

> We do ultimately have the power to give those grades. . . . [So we have to ask ourselves:] Why do you think people have to be able to do this? Why should they do this? Are you being rigid because you have power to be rigid or are there really good reasons for the kinds of decisions you make? And it doesn't mean, well, it also means recognizing that yes, you have the power to give students grades, but that doesn't mean that it's a good idea to just give away power by giving everyone As. There is still some meaning to grades at the university.

Jasmine attempted to reconcile her ideas about teaching and power with those expected through university policies.

Teachers expressed feeling many restrictions from working as professors or instructors in this institution. They struggled with reprioritizing their work to meet other professional demands that were expected of them. Brianne questioned:

> When am I going to be in a situation to really think about it for a long time? When am I going to read anything about feminist pedagogy? I don't know when it's going to happen. One wants a job,

one has to write a book. I mean there are many other things that one has to do, that I have to do. The kind of ideals that are represented by the idea of feminist teaching are hard—they're really hard. One wants to go, "Okay, well I want small groups, and I'll be nice, and I'll be a feminist teacher." It's way complicated. . . . It's just that it needs more time.

Another teacher talked about the expectations that her department had of the prioritization of her work, and the ways in which she attempted to work within those set priorities. When asked if her department supported her decision to work "only" 50 hours a week, Danielle said:

> I don't think it's a terrible disadvantage. That's as far as I can go. . . . But I think that a lot of it has to do with efficiency. I mean, if you can get your job done, if you do your committee assignments, if your teaching evaluations are good, if you're present at faculty meetings, if you participate actively in the intellectual and political life of the department, . . . they can't complain a whole lot. And if you're efficient, you can get that done in 50 hours a week.

At the same time, Danielle said of her teaching:

> It takes more time, but that's just my teaching, and I'm just buried with papers all the time. . . . I do a lot of grading. . . . So teaching is a constraint on my general career productivity. And there's no fooling yourself about that.

Teaching was seen, at least to Danielle, as getting in the way of her career advancement and tenure progression.

Gloria suggested a broader institutional perspective that conveyed a devaluing of teaching:

> The scholarship is the key in this institution. . . . You can be a mediocre teacher but an excellent researcher. You can't do excellent teaching and mediocre research. So I think those are the institutional rules—if we can't live by them, don't sign on.

Deborah's words accorded with Gloria's characterization of university priorities and practices:

> I don't feel as though I'm particularly watched except in the area of publication. I haven't had anyone visit my classroom and complain

that I'm not teaching properly. So I feel pretty free to do what I like, and I experiment all the time.

Even though Deborah's department didn't pay attention to her work except in terms of research and publication, the value that she placed on teaching encouraged her to keep trying to reflect on and improve her own practice. While teaching was valued in some departments, the larger institutional perspective of research as having a higher priority than teaching was prevalent throughout these interviews.

The norms and expectations of this particular university were seemingly understood by those who chose to work within these institutional boundaries. Those norms reinforced the preference for research over teaching and service. I learned that those who decided to step outside institutional boundaries to develop time- and energy-consuming feminist teaching practices often did so without a reward structure in place that would support their efforts and struggles.

INSTITUTIONAL EXPLICITNESS

Some teachers espoused a strategy to bring attention to and possibly begin to dismantle systemic structures while reshaping role expectations and norms. These teachers consciously chose to make their understandings and beliefs about higher education institutions explicit within classroom environments. As Brianne said,

When I turn around and look at the education institution it seems like a lot of it is sort of obfuscated. I look at my experience and I was largely confused about what was going on, why whoever was talking to me was talking to me, why the people in charge were in charge, and why and how decisions were being made. So a lot of what I'm interested in is just sort of foregrounding those kinds of institutional operations.

Additionally, teachers sought to problematize the assumptions and unstated political beliefs that supported institutional practices and norms. Alex talked about one of her roles as a teacher in her department:

I would also include in [a definition of teaching] advising, academic advising, career advising, and internships. I do it for everybody's students—I don't just do it for mine, because there are people who don't want to learn the system. . . . I have a lot of information and

> I make it a point to find out things that students need to know. . . .
> I think I have a responsibility to find out things that would be use-
> ful to them.

Eileen talked about her belief that it was important to be explicit about
the power that teachers have in the classroom in an attempt to be up-
front about institutionally granted power and authority as well:

> It's a lie when anybody pretends that they are not the teacher.
> That's not what's going on. And I think it's an abuse of power to
> say we are all going to be equals here. And I think that while, for a
> conversational style in my graduate seminar, I may put myself into
> this conversation as one of the participants, I don't think there is
> ever a moment where I should be pretending that I'm in an equal
> power relationship with people. I think it is better for that power to
> acknowledge it, to up front say, ''We operate within institutional
> constraints and this is one of them. This is a fact; this is a given of
> the situation.''

University norms affected the experiences that these feminist educators constructed and explored in classrooms. For example, Jasmine
said that she thought women's studies as a discipline was held to a
''very different standard'' than were other, more traditional disciplines.
And many others focused on their attempts to make explicit the responsibilities and roles that they perceived themselves to have within
their institutional environments. Brianne talked about class assignments
and educational philosophies that helped students to recognize and
function politically and ''effectively'' in institutional structures as well.
She said:

> I have this thing that you have to do this sort of informal academic
> drag—you have to have footnotes—I'm obviously sort of ambiva-
> lent and critical of the trappings of authority and that kind of dis-
> course, but at the same time you know you're not teaching in a Uto-
> pian space and so I think it's very valuable to write formal feminist
> criticism and then read it to a bunch of feminists first . . . so that is
> the kind of basic idea that I was working with a lot. [I'm looking]
> not so much at what the course was about in the larger sense, but
> the performance of it day to day or in the phrasing of things, or the
> enunciation of what was going on on a momentary basis.

Negotiating between using "academic drag" and drawing explicit attention to institutional norms and expectations was an ongoing process for Brianne. Teachers at colleges and universities were largely trained in similar institutions to those that they are now trying to reform or reconstruct. Advancing feminist beliefs in academic environments that are often not consonant with those values creates a challenging environment in which to practice.

Institutional expectations and assumptions of what education is to be and how it is to function largely affected some teachers' approaches. Through teachers' attempts to expose and consider institutional beliefs in relation to power between students and teachers, they made explicit underlying beliefs and understandings supporting and disrupting certain patterns of classroom interactions.

EXPANDING BOUNDARIES

Despite our efforts, for women, the experience of institutional education continues to have profound consequences: by our experience we know that in the intellectual community patriarchy lives, feminism is under siege, and the accomplishment of feminist pedagogy . . . is a struggle. I know by my own experience that for feminist intellectual workers— whether they be students or teachers—the academy is, for the most part, an uncomfortable and unwelcoming home.

(Lewis, 1993, p. 52)

I really look forward to a time in the week . . . when I know that intellectually I'll be stimulated and I'm going to receive something in return. I think in terms of one of the stresses of working with [other departmental responsibilities] is I think you tend to give a lot and it's not that they're not grateful and it's not that I don't learn anything, but it's an awful lot of giving in terms of what percentage of what you're giving and what you get. So in many ways my solace, if you will, intellectually is not only the time I have by myself but [also the time in class]—this class has become a wonderful place for me. And I realized that yesterday. I was thinking, oh good—I get to go to class.

(Mary Louise, Interview)

Feminist educators from a variety of disciplinary and departmental positions discussed with me their experiences of learning to negotiate on a continual basis the types of classroom teaching that they were able to construct given the institutional environments in which they were currently operating. While resistances to feminist practices in higher education abound in the literature, my purpose in this chapter was to discuss institutional factors that affected this group of feminist educators as they tried to implement their principles in and creatively construct their classrooms. Through this analysis, I hoped to better understand ways in which these educators sought to overcome or utilize those influences and resistances.

In some cases, these feminist educators recognized that they were working in particular structures and acknowledged that they were going to have to conform to those structures. In other cases, they worked to disrupt the preexisting expectations and norms to create teaching and learning environments that provided more options and opportunities for students who chose to participate and for themselves. Regardless, these teachers largely accepted that their teaching practices and beliefs were unavoidably influenced by institutional and disciplinary systems within which they were working. In some cases, such as in Julie's perception that her large class size enabled her to communicate with and teach more people, these factors and systems were seen as beneficial. In others, as with Danielle, teaching was perceived as having a negative affect on career productivity because of the professional, institutional, and departmental expectations with which teachers contend.

Teachers' experiences and understandings presented here suggest continual, albeit sometimes tentative, engagement of feminist discourse with higher education. This engagement can take many forms. For example, bell hooks (1994) suggested that the excitement or passion that feminist teachers brought to their classrooms could be understood as an act of transgression in the academy.

Harland Bloland (1995) believed that poststructural approaches have the potential to transgress current higher education structures, suggesting that they may lead educators in colleges and universities to consider "alternative" or "nontraditional" educational practices and perspectives in a significant way. In his words:

> It is not just a matter of responding with open arms to different dress and celebrations of new holidays, or of taking in new languages and literatures; it is dealing fairly but firmly with customs and values that have been morally repugnant to higher education. (p. 553)

Where, then, would poststructural approaches to feminist education within higher education institutions begin? The literature has already posed many starting points. Recognizing that educational institutions maintain, produce, and reproduce power structures through their systemic structures and role expectations may serve as a useful beginning. As Henry Giroux (1993) claimed,

> Educational institutions and the processes in which they engage are not innocent. Simply stated, schools are not neutral institutions designed for providing students with work skills or with the privileged tools of culture. Instead, they are deeply implicated in forms of inclusion and exclusion that produce particular moral truths and values. (p. 373)

Beginning to see and understand the lack of neutrality and the overt and covert presence of morals and assumptions in academic structures and in feminist practices is perhaps a first step in crafting a more conducive environment for feminist work in higher education.

Magda Gere Lewis (1993) encouraged feminist educators to analyze how systemic conditions restrict certain behaviors while enhancing others. In this case, she focused the analysis on women.

> As women in the academy, the terms under which we are required to speak and the conditions under which we cannot speak must become a focus for analysis as to how the academy might be used to disrupt the project of its own agenda. (p. 53)

Michelle Fine (1995) claimed that this process has already begun in important ways. In describing her beliefs, she stated, "Feminist scholars have interrupted the membrane of objectivity across the academy and in their respective disciplines, refusing containment and asking how feminist politics can and do play, explicitly and subversively, in our intellectual lives" (p. 14).

In each of these cases, feminist teaching was reiterative work. The processes through which feminist teaching carves a niche in higher education environments were not—and never will be—complete. Feminist teaching will constantly and continually be shaped by the processes, expectations, and structures that exist in our higher education institutions. At the same time, this relationship is reciprocal. Poststructuralism suggests that power is everywhere, operating through everything and all of us. That is, as feminist teaching and the principles that inform the various forms it takes are affected by institutional experiences, so too are those institutional experiences and structures undoubtedly affected by the principles that inform this and other intersections of feminism and higher education. Feminist discourses and the social forces embedded in institutions continually reshape each other's options and practices. bell hooks (1994) suggested: ''The academy is not paradise. But learning is a place where paradise can be created. The classroom, with all its limitations, remains a location of possibility'' (p. 207). These teachers do not exist in a vacuum. Their teaching, research, and service efforts are challenging and substantially contributing to the possibilities of feminist discourses in higher education environments.

PART II

Engaging Power: Critical Tensions and Resistances

A critique is not a matter of saying that things are not right as they are. It is a matter of pointing out on what kinds of assumptions, what kinds of familiar, unchallenged, unconsidered modes of thought the practices that we accept rest.

(Foucault, 1981/1988c, p. 154)

Power is something that I have a very ambivalent relationship with. On the one hand, not having ever had any and having felt so powerless growing up, it's heady in a way. On the other hand, having suffered from insensitive use and abuse of power, I am careful not to abuse it.

(Deborah)

Thus far, I have examined multiple social forces that interact with and inform feminist teaching practice and discourse. Additionally, I have emphasized that these forces are flexible, changing, and anchored in situation-bound contexts. I turn now to the ways in which power relations affect feminist teaching practices. While the social forces examined earlier were imbued with power, the power relations that I describe here take their form in the practices that exist and are disrupted within feminist teaching discourse. As such, the assumptions and norms of feminist teaching, as well as ways in which these norms were challenged, are the focus of this section.

As I am proposing norms and customary beliefs, I simultaneously hope to be "troubling" or questioning them as well. As Judith Hoover and Leigh Anne Howard (1995) proposed, "Postmodern philosophy urges us not toward order but toward multiplicity or even randomness" (p. 971). And Harland Bloland (1995) stated, "The modernist orientation is to resolve problems; the postmodern perspective not only points to the contradictions in discourses, but makes a virtue of preserving that essential tension" (p. 551). In relating my understandings of the complex positionings of what I am calling feminist teaching discourse, I hope to preserve the tension of which Bloland spoke.

I also am aware of the caution proposed by J. Daniel Schubert (1995) that a focus on normative beliefs may serve to perpetuate those beliefs. As he wrote,

> To focus on norms and values rather than practices is to ignore the local. The local is not a manifestation of universal norms and values. The social scientist who focuses on these more familiar notions is only legitimizing them and obfuscating the ways in which the power relations encoded in them can be changed. The point of progressive academic practice is not to legitimize such notions, but rather to show how they have come into existence and to transgress them. (p. 1004)

I hope, in this work, not to merely name and thereby reinforce norms and customary interactions in educational practices. Rather, I hope to identify and show possibilities both for resistance and for the establishment of new norms and structures created through specific and local practices and resistances. Through this process, I explore how "pedagogy seems to carry its own set of power relations" (Gore, 1997, p. 3). These power relations create a synergistic tension between the local and more common understandings in feminist teaching.

Feminist and poststructural scholars and educators have considered the implications of power in education generally (Burbules, 1986; Foucault, 1977/1988b) as well as in feminist or critical classrooms (Bright, 1987; Ellsworth, 1992, Gore, 1993; Lewis, 1993; Orner, 1992). They have framed power as crucial to poststructural analyses, insisting that power is everywhere working through everyone (Foucault, 1978); that it is strongly related to knowledge, difference, and language (Lather, 1991; Orner, 1992; Scott, 1990); and that resistance regularly exists *within* the exercise of power (Burbules, 1986; Munro, 1996). Jane Flax (1993) asserted, "Power is a productive force; discursive formations could not operate without it" (p. 39). And a teacher involved in my research emphasized the imperative of examining power relations within feminist teaching. As Julie told me,

> I think that [power] is the crux of everything that we're talking about. In fact, that is actually how I would describe feminist teaching—is whether someone is sufficiently aware of power dynamics in the world—that it's a core of who they are and what they teach. . . . And anything that you're teaching that's a part of disrupting the status quo is about power. It is, I think, the essence of what feminist analysis of the world is.

Conceptualizations and concerns relating to the power of feminist and poststructural scholars, as well as my own, have largely motivated my current line of questioning.

In feminist teaching practice, how is power conceptualized? How is it enacted? Jennifer Gore (1993) suggested an expansion of traditional understandings of power and, drawing on Foucault and Nicholas Burbules, wrote:

> Power is exercised or practiced, rather than possessed, and so circulates, passing through every related force. Students, as well as teachers, exercise power. In order to understand the operation of power contextually, we need to understand the particular points through which it passes. (p. 52)

Magda Gere Lewis (1993) added her understanding: "Power, as an embodied practice in relations of inequality, means being entitled to choose between a variety of meanings and further being entitled to decide when to hear and when not to hear the meanings articulated by another" (p. 166).

Because power is ubiquitous, enacted by and through all participants, it is difficult to discern. As Foucault (1977/1988b) claimed, "Power in the West is what displays itself the most, and thus what hides itself the best, . . . The relations of power are perhaps among the best hidden things in the social body" (p. 118). And yet the examination of these power relations and the norms that they establish and maintain is important because of their impact on our lives. Power relations are hidden, yet their effects are felt continually.

If power is exercised everywhere and through all who participate in any way in constructing feminist teaching practices, how does it find expression? As Bloland (1995) asserted, "Foucault is interested in power in terms of its results, or power at the point where it is wielded. This places his interest at the local level" (p. 531). Following Foucault's lead, I focus in this section on four specific—and yet at the same time intersecting and overlapping—instances or "arenas" of power interactions in the words and actions of teachers in this study and in feminist teaching literature.

Many educators have problematized the roles of various participants in shaping teaching practices. As discussed in part I, the interactions of multiple experiences and sources of power have continually shaped feminist teaching discourse. Here, though, I want to focus on ways in which those power relations have come to the fore around certain issues that have been prevalent in feminist teaching literature and discourse. These next four chapters are framed around the question, How does power, and resistance to that power, affect constructions of feminist teaching?

In chapter 5, I focus on power and resistance in relation to three teaching roles that participants repeatedly discussed in this research. I consider the question, What are crucial ways in which power is enacted and contested through variously positioned participants in feminist teaching discourse? In so doing, I propose that resistance, as framed through poststructural lenses, can be understood in different ways from those that predominate in feminist teaching literature. In chapter 6, the focus is on the ways in which knowledge is constructed and negotiated in feminist classrooms. I ask, What are participants' intents, values, norms, and beliefs as they enact the process of knowledge production and negotiation? In chapter 7, I turn to the ways in which differences are understood in feminist teaching practice through an examination of differences highlighted in my discussions and observations. I question, How does power affect and relate to the expression of difference? Finally, in chapter 8, I consider power as it relates to the choice of whether to speak or to be silent as well as to the ability to determine the communication of others. This analysis focuses on the questions, How are speech and silence incorporated into teaching and learning in feminist education environments? and, How do both speech and silence communicate meaning and indications of engagement? Throughout these chapters, I demonstrate how power emanates from multiple sources and has multiple effects in feminist classrooms. I further propose in each chapter tentative ideas for what poststructural feminist teaching discourse might suggest for future practice.

The categorical placement of data and interpretations in these sections is somewhat arbitrary in that there is often overlap between ideas in one section and their counterparts in another. This overlap is inevitable, I believe, because the negotiations that took place in these classrooms were not static or categorical themselves; nor were the teachers' viewpoints static or consistent across the group. The resulting richness of this data, therefore, cannot be fully captured in categories that are deemed separate and impartial. I urge the reader to consider overlaps and contradictions presented in this text.

CHAPTER 5

Powerful Places: (De)constructing Power and Resistance

Resistance is always a possibility, since what is offered can be withheld.
(Burbules, 1986, p. 101)

Feminist teaching is constantly changing. Multiple forces cause it to take a variety of shapes and forms. Subsequently, the practices of those who choose to participate in feminist teaching vary greatly. Students and teachers, women and men, people of many races, nationalities, sexualities, and abilities come together in feminist educational environments to participate in learning. Dichotomies become obscured; identities are multiple, shifting, and largely hidden from the explicit discourse of the class. Conflicts occur as those involved teach and learn from each other far more than the content listed on syllabi. Resistance is a part of learning.

To illustrate, I often conflicted with, or resisted, parental authority during my tumultuous teen years. The child was rebelling against rules and regulations that were set by "responsible adults" in the relationship. When I would complain, several years later, about how strict my parents had been, my father held up his hand, put it against mine and began pushing. The seemingly natural reaction on my part was to push back. His point was that when a certain level of pressure was placed on someone, resistance in some form will occur. That person will most likely begin to push back. Whereas he was trying to justify his parental decisions (because of the pressure that I apparently applied through my behavior), I believe that this example also has the potential to shed light on relationships of teachers and learners in higher education classrooms. Resistance is a two-sided phenomenon.

Feminist teaching literature has often framed resistance as *student* resistance to teachers' hopes and intentions for students (Deay & Stitzel, 1992; Dunn, 1993; Eichhorn et al., 1992; hooks, 1994; Lather, 1991;

Maher & Tetreault, 1994; Rakow, 1992). In other words, the work that needs to be done is set forth by teachers and either engaged with or resisted by students. Less frequently described is the manner in which students and teachers affect *each other's* learning and teaching practices and experiences. In turn, resistance is understood as student resistance to teachers' prescribed methods of learning. In Mimi Orner's (1992) words,

> Feminist and critical educators are clearly the ones who . . . can empower and interrogate because they are the ones who know. We are to believe that critical and feminist teachers have already dealt conclusively with their own inscription and involvement in oppressive power dynamics. . . . The only call for change is on the part of the students. The only people who get "worked over" are the students. The only call is for student voice. Critical and feminist teachers, we are to assume, have already found and articulate theirs. (p. 87)

In this chapter, I propose a different way of looking at power negotiations in student and teacher relationships. I suggest that both power and resistance can be more usefully conceptualized when the focus of analysis is on the tensions caused by social expectations that both students and teachers bring to their educational experiences.

Having examined several social forces that have served to shape feminist teaching discourse, I now turn to various points of tension for teachers as they crafted their practices. In chapter 3, I considered the ways in which those enacting feminist teaching attempted to be responsive to the students who were in their classrooms. Here, I refocus the question and ask instead, What are crucial ways in which power is enacted and contested by variously positioned participants in feminist teaching discourse? The analysis considers teachers' and students' prescribed or assumed uses of power and ways in which participants in feminist classrooms expanded the boundaries of "appropriate" power usage in their teaching and learning relationships through resisting and reestablishing certain patterns of interaction.

STUDENTS, TEACHERS, AND POWER: USES AND DISRUPTIONS

Students, institutions, and teachers themselves held expectations for the behaviors, customs, and uses of power in classroom teaching. To be sure, these expectations were not always in line with each other. Often, teaching practice, as a site where these expectations and norms were contested and conflicted, varied greatly. At times, teachers whom

I interviewed and observed were fully aware that they were following a set of expectations other than those formally set out by the institution. They enacted a power (ironically, often institutional power that operated through them) to call for a disruption of that same power system or of other social norms and customs. I frame this section in terms of practices that were acknowledged and contested in classroom discourse. In each section, I discuss multiple ways in which those norms were resisted and contested, and suggest that new ways of interacting sometimes shifted normative power expectations.

Teachers as Experts on Learning

One educational custom that I came to understand as contested terrain in feminist teaching discourse was that which set up teachers to be experts not only in teaching and topical knowledge, but also in methods of learning. In this study, several teachers entered classrooms viewing themselves as experts in students' learning. Many shared Nancy Schniedewind's (1983) perspective: "I don't have a totally egalitarian classroom. I take more leadership and have more power than any of the students. I have found that students need an arena in which to *learn* to take responsibility for themselves and the group" (p. 265). Teachers in this study often believed that they should take charge of the teaching and learning methods that framed their classroom discourses.

As I observed Andrea's class, I noticed that the discussion was very teacher focused and teacher directed, but Andrea maintained a wide opening for student input by asking many questions and explicitly encouraging student participation. Rosa's class was very teacher directed as well. Primarily through Rosa did students respond to each other's comments. In other words, if students had a response to Rosa, the reading, or another student, they would raise their hands and wait to be called on. Rosa determined the content to be wrestled with and discussed.

Gloria maintained this expert teacher role in her class at certain points as well. In a conversation about education (12 April), she described her belief that "[education] is not just about sitting around and feeling good. . . . There's a gap between what [students] know and what you want them to know, and your job is to find a connection." In discussing the assignment options from which students could choose, Gloria (22 March) told the class, "Make sure you and I have talked about what you're going to do [if you're choosing a certain option]. . . . It's rarely been problematic, but I just want to make sure." Additionally, Gloria regularly explained the purposes of her pedagogical choices in the classroom. These descriptions suggested that she had thought extensively about teaching and learning and had something of potential value to offer students in that regard.

Mary Louise demonstrated a similar competence in the area of teaching and learning in a different way. She encouraged students to "do what they needed" on assignments and only reluctantly responded to student requests that she further describe details of what she expected from assigned class projects. Further, after an intense class discussion (25 April), she told the class that because of student responses, she now "felt validated" about having chosen those particular readings. Mary Louise was certainly well versed in both teaching and learning techniques and practices. Yet her enactment of her knowledge took on this different shape, as she explicitly relied, at least partly, on student feedback for validation of her educational choices.

Several teachers in my study realized that they drew on their institutional roles and the power that accompanied those roles to assume this expert teaching position. In one instance, Sharon said:

> When I go into the classroom, I am not a facilitator. I am an orchestra leader. But [students] all have instruments and they have their own autonomous thing. But I had put the syllabus together, so in that sense . . . it is not a nonhierarchical event in classrooms. And I think if one pays too much attention to trying to say it is not [a hierarchy], then you kind of undermine what happens.

Another teacher used the metaphor of an orchestrator to describe her role as well. In Rosa's words,

> I tend not to draw attention to classroom dynamics. I'm so aware of them, but I don't want [students] to be self-conscious about them. And I think that's mostly my job as a teacher, to try to orchestrate so that it makes it more comfortable for them to do this. But I tend not to want to draw attention to classroom dynamics, whether they're going well or not.

Through taking total responsibility for and control of classroom dynamics and processes, these teachers began to set up a custom or norm that prescribed their roles as experts of students' learning.

What roles does this set up for students? What types of practices are available to or expected from students when teachers are seen as having an expert authority to "manage" learning that occurs in classrooms? What are students' customary roles within this dualistic understanding of teacher and student? I propose that setting teachers up as experts in learning, with an ultimate claim to the production of learning environments and students' participation within those environments, allows only a very narrow space within which students can explore and craft learning on their own.

This dichotomous relationship (between teachers and students) urged students very quickly to make choices about the degree to which they were willing to engage in a place where they were not seen as primary shapers of discourse. Jasmine commented on the resistance or disengagement of students in her class. She described her efforts to engage students and her subsequent reactions when they continued to refuse participation:

> I try to keep going the way I'm going and if they want to sit there and sulk for an hour while we have a discussion of [an issue], then fine. If they don't care about [the topic], whatever. If they don't want to debate that or listen to that or think about that, I'm not going to waste my energy.

The disengagement of some of these students seemed beyond the control of the teacher.

Ruth noticed a disengagement of students in her class as well and explored her understandings of the reasons for that lack of participation. In her words,

> I try to help [students] understand that they can theorize, because many students of mine don't believe that. They think that theory is useless, for one thing. They think that it comes from outside and the outside doesn't know the inside. [Through a journaling exercise] they begin to see for the first time that it's possible for them to see themselves as building and understanding a particular set of values and then looking at a higher issue or question.

Teachers often made judgments about classroom activities and events based on their own perceptions of what would be most valuable for students. Yet, expectations of students in their classes also influenced ways in which teachers tried to craft classroom environments. Chris described her role and the ways that students normalized her to perform a certain function within the classroom:

> Part of my role is to generate thought-provoking questions; and part of my role also is to keep the discussion organized and fo-

cused, because the discussion can go all over the place. I've had students complain to me that they were in a 50-minute class where it's been all discussion and they don't know what they got out of it. So I see a role to keep things focused and to bring us back to the topic if things stray.

Because students wanted to keep "on track" and concretely "know" what they learned from class discussion, they expected Chris to keep the focus of class on what students saw as relevant class topics.

When teachers chose to create environments that were not "typical" or "traditional," they also ran the risk of having students who, for myriad reasons, resisted the classroom environments that resulted. Deborah talked about resistance from her students in that they wanted the "expert" (Deborah) to talk, rather than to allow time for all participants to discuss a topic at hand, as was Deborah's intent. Brianne discussed the difficulty of knowing when to disrupt student expectations for teacher-student interactions and when to allow them to remain unchallenged in her classrooms. And finally, Eileen talked about the reactions that her students had to the classrooms that she attempted to craft:

> Some feel like it's a ghetto, that it's not being carried out in their other classrooms. So what is the point of raising this consciousness if there's not a place for it to carry through? It's just annoying. . . . [Sometimes] a person can take [something] back to other settings. Or even that you know you have one place to go. You don't have to have it everywhere. Some people just can't wait to get out of there, and they may never want to come back to a classroom like that again.

Throughout my study, teachers and students recognized that developing classroom structures most conducive to learning in the midst of conflicting ideas about educational purposes was a point of conflict and, often, resulted in constant negotiation of the beliefs that guided classroom practices.

Whereas all teachers realized that they must participate in shaping classroom learning environments and perform in a customary or expected way to some extent, several challenged themselves and their students to form a more reciprocal relationship in developing the structures of their classes. Some teachers wanted students to take more control over their own learning and their learning environments. For example, on the first day of class, Rae and her students set up guidelines for participation in the class that they would be creating together. While she contributed significantly to this classroom process, she brought to the attention of students that they also had both stances on and stakes in the ways that the classroom discourse would develop and proceed. Rae, and several others, also sought informal comments from students throughout the semester on how well the learning environment was meeting students' needs and expectations. In this way, these teachers began to disrupt the custom that placed teachers as the primary authorities on learning processes in classrooms.

Brianne described her difficulty in examining her position as a teacher and, more specifically, that of being an expert on students' learning. In so doing, she emphasized multiple expectations that were being made of her and her role, and deliberated about her response:

> I guess one of the things that is a real conflict for me is how much time to spend being reflexive about teaching. I mean, I think that wanting to radicalize the organization of the classroom is a great impulse, but I'm wary of it becoming sort of a fetish and limiting the practical work of the course—given that the whole system is not changing all at once, that there is a limit to the amount of internal focus that you can have about that kind of thing.

Brianne struggled with her use of limited class time and energy to examine and create classroom discourses that incorporated views of students. Although seeing that process as valuable, she nevertheless was torn over the proper role of herself as a teacher.

Although I have set up this analysis to compare and contrast perspectives on teachers as experts of learning, I have simultaneously attempted to show how this *expert* status is contested by both teachers and students who believe that classroom environments have the potential to be more inclusive, with all participants explicitly shaping learning environments. What is at issue here? If students refuse to "engage" with teachers' prescribed classroom activities, are they really no longer a part of shaping the discourse? I would argue that their disengagement is as powerful as would be their exacting response to teachers' calls for participation.

From participants in this research and literature, I have learned that some of those involved in feminist teaching discourse often set themselves up as experts of students' learning. And many students held tightly onto teachers' enactment of that role, hoping to have someone other than themselves manage what was important for them to know. Thus, an attempt to deconstruct normative barriers along this axis may be met with resistance by those playing a variety of roles. For those who are not comfortable within this norm, however, the boundaries can be articulated, struggled with, and, perhaps, shifted.

Teachers as Empowerers

Many scholars have problematized the existence of power in classrooms (Ellsworth, 1992; Gore, 1990, 1993; Jipson, 1995; Morgan & Rhoden, 1995; Munro, 1996; Weiler, 1988). Some have argued that not only does the image of empowerment falsely present a vision of developing equality (Smith, 1994), but it also leaves largely unproblematized the assumption that, in classrooms, teachers know what is best or most useful for students (Burbules, 1986). As Gore (1990) suggested,

> In attempts to empower others we need to acknowledge that our agency has limits, that we might "get it wrong'" in assuming we know what would be empowering for others, and that no matter what our aims or how we go about "empowering," our efforts will be partial and inconsistent. (p. 63)

When power is conceptualized as existing only in the hands of teachers, with students needing to be empowered in order to "receive" power, many such concerns rise to the fore.

The belief that teachers had a great deal of power to shape classroom discourse was often contested in feminist teaching. This understanding of teachers' power often led the teachers with whom I spoke to consider the ways in which they could both acknowledge their power and, subsequently, use it to *empower* students in their classrooms. For example, Vicki expressed her desire to empower students by providing an environment that allowed them to develop knowledge:

> I think that is very deceptive to pretend that the professor doesn't have a certain kind of power that the students don't have. I would much prefer to acknowledge it and then try to use it fairly and for the ultimate purpose of empowering students, by giving them an experience that allows them to develop their own knowledge bases, their own ways of thinking.

Other teachers agreed that they possessed a certain degree of institutionally granted power, and that they hoped to use that power for the purposes of empowering or sharing power with students.

Within a custom in which it was understood that teachers maintained control and the ability to empower others, what roles were available to students? Students were seen as those with less power, and a greater need to be empowered. Students were assumed to be in need of power, which suggested that they had somehow previously been denied the opportunities to operate within or from a powerful position. This argument presents a quandary for teachers' practices in their classrooms.

Teachers' institutionally granted power was continually questioned and disrupted by various events and belief systems, customs and norms, that were played out in classrooms. As discussed earlier, several teachers talked about their status as women in positions of authority and suggested that students' expectations of female teachers were different from those that they held of male teachers. Others felt that because of communication styles of certain students, their power had been lessened. Sarah described a time when a male student had monopolized classroom conversations, adding,

> I have felt powerless. I have felt powerless this semester. I've always felt relatively good about my ability to kind of manage conversations—to be able to help people shift gears or to move along a conversation that has gotten stuck, by inserting a question that might get things moving, or being able to change the subject. And I haven't been able to do that this semester. And that's [a] feeling of powerlessness.

Because the classroom discourse wasn't proceeding in a way that Sarah and many other students were comfortable with, Sarah felt a lack of power that was contradictory to the norms that instate teachers with both power for themselves and power to empower others. Students in these classrooms brought their own sources of power and resistance to their learning conditions. Based on multiple statuses with which they identified or were identified, students were granted or assumed power in ways that perhaps teachers could not or chose not to assume. In other words, the "teacher-student" status indicator was only one measure among many of assumed power and authority. These measures alternately interacted with, magnified, and diminished each other.

One teacher described her difficulty in determining how to understand the multiple forms and sources of power that are available to, and operate through, teachers. Eileen asked difficult questions about the ways in which she, and others, can negotiate their sources of power and use them their intended ways:

> Women are just occupying jobs now that have power with them. And how are you going to negotiate [that] and what models are

you going to follow? And . . . what about the kinds of power, any kind of power, that you can't make go away? How are you going to conduct yourself within them? . . . There are kinds of White power that accrue in the position that I occupy. As a perceived White person. How am I going to negotiate that power? . . . How am I eventually [going to] be a person who has power over certain kinds of other tenured positions? How do you negotiate power that accrues with particular positions that we occupy?

How, then, do teachers begin to understand or even recognize multiple sources of power that they influence and are influenced by? What sources of power can teachers draw upon and resist in order to enact power dynamics in conscious, deliberate, and educationally useful ways? The tensions caused by these conflicting practices continue to trouble feminist teaching discourse.

I learned that teachers often felt a responsibility to empower students with whom they worked, but that they struggled with understanding how to do that within fluctuating and unstable power relations. What is empowerment? Is there a way to empower others without assuming a "higher" power status, at least temporarily, for oneself? If students are empowered to resist, in this case, a feminist agenda or academic practice, is that acceptable to those espousing feminist educational principles?

The "object" of empowerment, I believe, cannot be left out of this analysis. What is the purpose of empowerment and who knows and establishes that purpose? Why is there not a parallel discourse that focuses on how students can empower teachers? In our multiple positions, which taken together in dynamic conversation locate each individual as part of many discourses, we and the discourses that we constitute establish tentative and temporary relations of power and empowerment.

Teachers as Monitors

Another role that was expected, and seemingly required, of teachers in this academic setting was that of monitor. This monitoring function was used to determine "normal" or "acceptable" functioning on the part of students in relation to class material and student identity. This function was not uncontested, however. Many teachers spoke of myriad deliberations in considering their roles in monitoring or participating in the surveillance of students, and questioned institutional and academic customs that put them in these positions.

One example of this monitoring custom took the form of evaluation practices. Traditional evaluation leads to a valuing of students' work in differential ways, often as determined and structured by the teacher. This evaluation then determines the quality of students' practices in that classroom. Many teachers in this research talked about their dilemmas in evaluating students and simultaneously pointed out that it was a concern that students had as well.

Tonika talked about the ways in which she viewed evaluation processes and tried to work within those processes to achieve her desired educational goals:

> I, for one, hope that I never abuse that [evaluative] power, but I'm always aware that I have that power and that students always also do their work cognizant that I have the power to determine how they will do—whether good or bad. So once it seemed to me that it was not possible to strip the classroom completely of the power dynamic between the teacher and the student, then to be the best kind of teacher that I would like to be, I continually am trying to reconfigure, How can I teach without that power dynamic getting in the way of students' performance? How can I teach them without dampening the creativity of my students because they're afraid of doing something that I might not approve of [or] because they're afraid that I will give them a grade that they don't want to get if they do something that I disapprove of? So my job has been, over time, to try to find ways to neutralize that power. I can't get rid of it. But I try to neutralize it so that it doesn't intimidate students. So that it doesn't make them feel that they don't have something to offer.

Another teacher echoed Tonika's realization that students were very aware that they were being judged not only on their written work, but also on their class participation and interactions. Deborah said:

> I sat in on one group and made one student uncomfortable. She said, "I was just about to say something nasty and negative." I told her it didn't matter—to go ahead. And she did, but I think the group felt they had to perform for me. They feared that I would judge or grade their responses and were uncomfortable with my coming down from the podium to join their group.

Even when Deborah attempted to participate and listen to students' discussions without the intention of grading, monitoring, or evaluating, students continued to perceive her as being in that customary evaluative role.

In this "normal" or "customary" relationship, then, students were viewed as persons who needed to be watched and conditioned or normalized so that they would perform certain acceptable functions in the classroom and, presumably, in the societies and communities that they would eventually populate. Many teachers who participated in my research spoke of the ways in which they tried to make clear and, perhaps, diminish their own power in relation to this monitoring role. They wanted students to take part in choosing their own preferred ways of meeting institutional requirements. For example, Rae asked students to assign themselves grades for their participation in classroom discussions. In doing so, she allowed them to monitor themselves in this one aspect. Cheryl graded students based on a "weighted" scale, through which students could determine which classroom tasks they wanted her to consider most seriously in assigning a course grade. Whereas she considered and provided feedback on all work, students could ask that their strengths, rather than their weaknesses, be monitored most closely for evaluation purposes. In other words, students could determine the direction of the teachers' evaluative "gaze."

Gloria and Mary Louise both attempted to disrupt more common notions of monitoring in their classes. First, they provided many participation options from which students could choose so that, at least in terms of formal evaluation, they could decide what types of activities they would like to have judged or observed. As Gloria (1 February) commented to the class when we regrouped after being in small group discussions, "I purposefully went into my office because I don't trust myself not to talk . . . and I realize that I have to fill out the grade sheet. So I stayed in my office and answered a phone call and did some other things. It's not that I didn't want to be by you." Both teachers also provided extensive feedback, rather than grades, throughout the semester.

From observing Mary Louise's teaching practices, I came to understand another function of monitoring students or participating in their surveillance. Regularly, Mary Louise would look not only at the person speaking but also at everyone else around the room. It seemed if she were monitoring the class not in an individually evaluative way, but rather in a way so that if something happened that needed attention—perhaps in the form of a student wanting to speak, or someone disengaging from the group discussion—she would be aware of and able to address that. This form of monitoring took on less of an evaluative focus and shifted to one that sought to include and respect potential contributions of all students.

Nearly all teachers spoke of monitoring or evaluating as a point of contestation and conflict in their teaching. Brianne asked questions that resounded in many other teachers' words:

> I try not to fall into that trap of saying we have this sort of open honest space in which my institutional power doesn't matter—[that] it goes away. That is definitely a temptation when I start thinking about, What is teaching about? What am I doing? How can I do it differently? And I think a real strong temptation [is] to take up a stance that seems to be outside the institution and to ignore things like you know the power of grading and surveillance kind of stuff and pretend that that isn't going on. So it's complicated.

This temptation of which Brianne spoke was one that many teachers felt. However, they realized the danger—both to themselves and to students—of ignoring the custom that dictated the terms of their work as teachers.

EMERGING PRACTICES AND CRITIQUES OF POWER

> I actually think it is possible to change things in the classroom and that a little bit of itsy, bitsy change in the classroom just might carry over beyond the classroom. In the best of circumstances, it does. But it happens not nicely and sweetly and with melodious harmony. It happens uneasily because it is discomforting. If I walk into a classroom, I know what is expected of me. I know how I can function in authority. I know how I can function as a teacher-type. My thoughts, as a student in the classroom, [are that] I know about what I have to do if I want to get a good grade, if I want to survive that class, survive the undergrad programs, survive the graduate program. I know what that means. Even if I think I'm an exception, I know what that means on some level; I may get better or worse at the performing level, . . . but it is some kind of stability, so that part of the way to change the classroom is the challenge in that area of stability. . . . I actually think that one by one we individually help each other reach . . . to change the structures of institutions as well.
>
> (Alea)

This chapter has contemplated various tensions in the classroom structures and resulting interactions with which both teachers and students in feminist classrooms contended. For the most part, teachers were tentatively and problematically constructed as experts in learning processes and as empowerers of students both by themselves and the expectations of others. Further, teachers monitored students' classroom activity, often discussing their experiences of conflict as they did so. Just as implicit norms and assumptions undergirded traditional and accepted or expected classroom practices, so too were there norms implied by feminist teaching practice. These norms, however, were not stable. Accordingly, in the rest of the chapter, I speculate on the multiple power-related practices that have been, or have the potential to be, developed within the contestations of feminist practices described above that fall within a feminist poststructural teaching discourse.

First, in my view, a feminist poststructural teaching discourse pays close attention to socially reinforced relationships that affected and were reproduced in classroom discourse. Those involved would seek to change relationships or assumptions about appropriate communication and interaction that were based on preconceived notions and understandings of participants' own and others' differences, while simultaneously realizing their limited ability to do so. Eileen[1] talked about her understandings:

> I think something that certainly differentiates feminist pedagogy from other pedagogies is the attention to the dynamics of the group in the classroom. To be not only always watching what is going on in the group, and aiding what's going on with the group, but also constantly aware of the ways in which power plays in the classroom. And also the ways in which, as the person with the official institutional power, there are certain things that you can do to intervene early on or in advance, and make slight shifts that may be only brief—they're only for the length of the semester—but they allow the students a hiatus in power dynamics that otherwise operate in their lives. They can have a slightly different classroom relationship.

Eileen emphasized her belief that she could try to make social interactions in the classrooms in which she participated somehow different from those that continually affected her and students in other environments.

Mary Louise seemed to shift power relations in a way that was not often found in classrooms. In my field notes of the fourth class meeting (14 February), I wrote:

> Notable is that Mary is really taking a back-seat role to what happens in class. She is no longer necessarily the center of attention.

Some people continue to look at her when they talk, but not many, as a general rule. . . . Mary is definitely a strong member, but not the only member who is leading us through this process.

Both Mary Louise and Eileen shared a hope that they could create classroom cultures that set up more inclusive and mutually shaped educational environments in a variety of ways.

Second, and closely related, a feminist poststructural teaching discourse continually problematizes the nature of power enacted through teachers and students in the form (or guise) of empowerment. Empowerment of students was a frequent topic of discussion in both literature and my interviews. Often, teachers in this study problematized the notion of empowerment in its traditional form. In other words, whereas teachers still sought to influence power relations in their classrooms, thereby creating more equitable environments, some realized both that they did not have exclusive power that they could "give" students, nor were students always anxious to "take" power in the ways that teachers intended.

Jennifer Gore (1990) suggested that empowerment generally implies an agent of empowerment, a notion of power as property, and some vision, end state, or goal. The teacher, then, becomes an agent of empowerment by giving power to students to achieve a purpose or goal, usually designated by the agent of empowerment. While Patti Lather (1991) described empowerment as something one does for oneself, empowerment remains problematic in many ways. Elizabeth Ellsworth (1992) described the dangers that she perceived in conceptualizing teachers as empowering students:

> Strategies such as student empowerment and dialogue give the illusion of equality while in fact leaving the authoritarian nature of the teacher/student relationship intact. "Empowerment" is a key concept in this approach, which treats the symptoms but leaves the disease unnamed and untouched. (p. 98)

Eileen added her concerns: "I think that there are moments in which for reasons that are both trustworthy and untrustworthy, one has a sense of empowerment." She further considered that those being empowered may not be fully aware of the intentions and motivations of those doing the empowering, or even those creating the environment in which persons may feel or be empowered.

The reinforcement of relationships—such as empowering ones— that set up those with and without power, serves to maintain dichotomies based on statuses or identities but fails to take into account multiple ways in which power acts and interacts within and around all classroom participants. During this study, Gloria and Mary Louise in many ways sought to disrupt those dichotomies by offering opportunities for participation in both in-class exercises and in conferences and publication opportunities outside of class. Some students in these classes saw themselves as contributors in this way as well and brought similar opportunities to the attention of other class members.

As Gore (1993) suggested, it is difficult to figure out one's role in a classroom if one is viewing power relations in *either/or* terms, as haves and have nots. Rather, a recognition of multiple sources of power, empowerment, and oppression—all creating dissonance and tendencies for resistance within our belief systems and understandings of others—could help teachers and students craft roles for themselves within fluctuating power dynamics. Although it was not explicitly conveyed in these words, I understood the practice of "troubling empowerment" to be evident in several teachers' practices examined in this study, and believe that it should remain a topic of deliberation in feminist poststructural teaching discourse.

Third, a poststructural feminist teaching discourse attempts to examine and discuss the meanings of teachers' own multiple sources of power and resistance. As I learned from my study, feminist teaching discourse was conflicted, as some teachers were torn between their need to participate in class interactions from a predefined location of "teacher" and their desires to somehow break the preconceived roles of what that participation might mean. They recognized that they had a certain degree of power, but wanted to minimize the harm (maximize the educational good) of that power. As Brianne said,

> One thing that I think about a lot, and sort of spent a lot of time obsessing about last semester in talking to colleagues, is the conflict between wanting to have the most volitional free-discussion structure possible. And at the same time not wanting to pretend that I'm not listening differently than anyone else in the room. And that I'm being compensated differently than everyone else for my participation. . . . I have one colleague [who] argues very strongly that, in many cases, the tradition of teaching is to obfuscate or confuse what is going on in the classroom. That just being clear about what [power] is, [and] where it is you are using power [is against tradition]. What is it you are asking for? What is it that you are doing sort of on a moment-to-moment basis? Being clear about that and perhaps more forceful or organized is in some ways potentially

more liberating or helpful to certain students than a more passive
[role].

Brianne sought to clarify her use of power so that she could be more
helpful to students. Teachers' explicit reexamination and tentativeness
of their relation to power remain important deliberations in creating a
feminist poststructural teaching discourse.

Fourth, much literature and several teachers in this study discussed
the possibilities for and opportunities found in resistance. Patti Lather
(1991) has suggested that opportunities for growth and understandings
of teachers' own "impositional tendencies" may be found in students'
resistances to teachers' prescribed classroom practices. Additionally,
Magda Gere Lewis (1990) urged, "As feminist teachers we need to look
closely at the psychosexual context within which we propose the feminist alternative and consider the substance of why women may genu-
inely wish to turn away from the possibilities it offers" (p. 484). A
feminist poststructural teaching discourse conceptualizes resistance not
merely as subversive, but also as powerfully productive when enacted
by both teachers and students.

What, then, can feminist teachers learn from resistance? What are
points through which teachers and students contest each other in efforts
to shape environments that are more conducive to their own customs
and norms and which meet their needs? Is not critical thinking a form of
resistance? Is not prohibiting sexist or racist language in classrooms a
form of resistance? In fact, Dennis Carlson (1995) suggested that "[Fou-
cault's] image of a postmodern democratic society is one in which there
is a continuous bringing into question of power relations and a continuous subversion, resistance, and demystification of power" (p. 356).
What can we learn from continuous resistance in teaching and learning?

In redefining power and resistance as emanating through students
and teachers, an analysis of classroom relations is opened up for mutual
learning and defining of practices that are perhaps unique to particular
classroom environments. As Nicholas Burbules (1986) suggested,

> We must see our methods of determining interests, and power relations, as
> potential power issues themselves. Certainly a major rationale for assum-
> ing power over others, or justifying it to them, is the presumption that one
> knows better and can best serve their interests. . . . We can inquire of
> others what they believe their interests to be, but we can also question
> them; we can pose alternative versions of their interests and disclose incon-
> sistencies or ambiguities in their own versions. . . . In the end we may
> convince them or be convinced ourselves. (p. 99)

Resistance, and lessons learned from tensions it supports, may provide useful understandings of ways that students and teachers can craft their own classroom cultures based both on contestation and mutual principles. It can be pictured not as something to be "overcome" or "gotten through." Rather, in feminist poststructural teaching discourse, classroom resistances can be analyzed in terms of the questions that they pose, the tensions that they bring to the fore, and the alternatives that they suggest for building new structures and power relations within educational communities.

CHAPTER 6

Situated Texts: Negotiating Knowledge and Knowing

> The powers of creating and dispensing knowledge in our universities are at base only reflections of, and continuing guarantees of, powers in our social institutions at large.
>
> (Maher, 1985, p. 46)

Teaching and learning arguably form the core of any educational experience. Yet as previously discussed, the act of choosing methods through which teaching and learning take place remains one of contested meanings. Just as is the case in other power-related practices, those who are committed to feminist teaching have multiple understandings of what it means to engage with/in knowledge negotiations.

Much feminist teaching literature grapples with knowledge that is created in and forms the content for classroom experiences in higher education. Feminist educators have not only critiqued the partiality of current knowledge bases (Boxer, 1985; Gore, 1993; Howe, 1977; Robinson, 1973); they have also attempted to rebuild knowledge and knowledge-making processes that incorporated a wider range of perspectives and experiences.

Some feminist perspectives closely align themselves with feminist poststructural understandings of knowledge and meaning. Knowledge, in poststructuralism, is very closely related to power (Gore, 1993; Middleton, 1993). As Jane Flax (1993) argued,

> Postmodernist investigations . . . encourage us to pay more attention to the varying conditions under which conflicting truth claims can be put forward or resolved. We cannot understand knowledge without tracing the effects of the power relations that simultaneously enable and limit the possibilities of discourse. (p. 138)

It is this power-knowledge relationship that determines whose experiences and whose knowledges become recognized and acted upon. Accepted knowledges, then, vary over time and depend on social contexts. Therefore, "objectivity," or being able to remove oneself or one's "biases" totally from one's understandings or perceptions, is considered an impossibility. This stance leads to a questioning of the possibility of anyone ever being able to explain or describe "reality" as it is typically understood. Thus, feminist poststructuralism acknowledges the varied realities presented from each person's own locations, as influenced by their experiential backgrounds.

In this chapter, I look at knowledge negotiation processes through a poststructural problematization of knowledge construction and meaning. I discuss what I learned about ways in which teachers in my study created spaces for and struggled within this relationship of negotiating knowledge and knowing in higher education classrooms. I use the term *negotiation* to characterize the constant redefinitions of knowledge in many forms as it is developed through tensions between and contributions of class content, students, teachers, and other social factors. Throughout, I question, What are participants' intents, values, norms, and customs in the ways that they view the process of knowledge production and negotiation? And further, What power structures support and contest the expression of resulting practices? What types of knowledges are validated in this process?

CLASSROOM KNOWLEDGE NEGOTIATION: CUSTOMS AND DISRUPTIONS

The feminist teachers with whom I spoke often had expectations for the participation of students both in terms of bringing various types of knowledge to classroom environments and contributing to knowledge negotiating activities during class sessions. In this section, I describe those expectations and struggles that occurred when some class members' expectations were different from others. As in the last chapter, I present this analysis by focusing on practices or philosophies that were contested in classroom discourse. More specifically, I have chosen to include here a focus on teachers and students as teachers and learners, teachers and students as critical thinkers and challengers, teachers as classroom managers, and teachers and students as knowledge contributors.

Teachers and Students as Teachers and Learners

> If knowledge needs to be conceived as produced in exchange, so too must
> all agents in its active production be conceived as producers, the divisions
> between theorising, writing, teaching and learning be dissolved.
>
> (Lusted, 1986, p. 5)

Albeit in differing ways, teachers and students were expected to
both learn from and teach each other in many of these feminist classroom environments. In other words, traditional roles of students and
teachers were challenged as classroom participants were expected, to
varying degrees, to perform both roles in knowledge negotiations. Elizabeth Ellsworth (1992) suggested that

> the literature explores only one reason for expecting the teacher to "re-
> learn" an object of study through the student's less adequate understand-
> ing, and that is to enable the teacher to devise more effective strategies for
> bringing the student "up" to the teacher's level of understanding. (p. 98)

Contrary to these understandings, several teachers with whom I interacted in this research claimed that they sought to learn from students
because they thought that students' knowledge was valuable for their
own continued learning.

Teachers learning from students. Teachers learned from students in
many different ways. For example, Gloria often asked students to critique her work, commenting in one class (15 February), "Really I'm not
thin-skinned. This is what you're supposed to be learning how to do.
It's already accepted for publication, so you can't hurt me, you can only
help me." Through an observation in Andrea's class, I realized that she
also sought to learn from students. After struggling on her own with
how to draw a model that they were grappling with on the chalkboard,
Andrea turned to the students and said, "We're having a little problem
here." Apparently, students had become accustomed to being asked to
contribute and struggle with these concepts previously because almost
immediately, four students' hands went up and Andrea began asking
people to describe how they would solve the problem.
    Another example of some teachers' understandings of their own
learning in classroom knowledge negotiation processes was that they
were open to being questioned and taught by students. In most cases,
teachers talked about their desire for students not to simply acquiesce to

the knowledge presented or to teachers' perspectives. I observed that often teachers would not give their perspectives immediately because they wanted students to form and feel free to express their own views before hearing those of the teacher. Many teachers talked about how much they valued perspectives that students had contributed during their classes. Chris expressed her appreciation of student contributions through this example:

> If we were talking about [a content area], and I had come to a point where I was stumped, I had all these people who knew the answers. And sometimes when we are doing feminist theories, some of the students have had actually more feminist theory courses in humanities than I have. So, I would just say, "This is how much I know about feminist theory. Now what can you add?" . . . I think it's my obligation to structure what the discussion is as I see the important topics in [this area] and to provide what I know about those topics and then go on to what the students can provide in the discussion.

Julie talked about a specific classroom event that drastically affected the way she conceptualized both her field and the work that she wanted to do within it for many subsequent years.

> It was a semester where I learned so much from watching my students listen to that lecture and what they did with it, it has totally changed my life. From that moment on, first of all I couldn't believe that I hadn't seen that [a certain topic] was a key . . . issue. . . . That's definitely something that I learned from my students. I had never thought about it. It was just watching what happened in their response to [a guest's] lecture and listening to discussion and stuff that made me know that I had to teach in a real different way. I mean, that's the most obvious [time I learned from students] because it's such a big part of my life now. But until—and I can literally remember the day—until that happened to me, it was a connection I hadn't made.

Both Julie and Chris believed that students' participation in and contribution to their classrooms had enriched their own education and the classroom environment that they were able to provide for other students.

Mary Louise stated similar views, but insisted that students were part of a learning "circle," rather than merely additive to her own knowledge. In an interview, she told me:

> At the end of the class, I've really had the opportunity to think about my teaching. I think of different ways of teaching. . . . It's sort of a self-feeding thing that goes on because we have excellent graduate students . . . and they push us as teachers and they push our research and ask questions of that. So then the work that is done here in terms of teaching and research is different than it would have been. And it's a circle.

The circle that Mary Louise described was enacted in her classroom in several ways. For instance, she encouraged participants to engage with each other in discussion, rather than deferring to her for the "answer." She also remained flexible to changing her interpretations if challenged by other students, commenting in one class (14 February), "I'm not countering or saying that your interpretation is faulty in any way. I just need to go back and read it again because I didn't read it that way."

The student-as-teacher section of this circle of learning was further demonstrated by a practice that Mary Louise continued throughout the semester. She regularly brought a set of her own notes, consisting of questions that she had about the assigned readings and quotes from materials outside of the class reading, which she handed out to students. Students would also contribute their questions to a collective list that was written on a chalkboard. As Mary Louise handed out her questions during the second class (31 January), she told class participants: "This is not the focus, but it's some of the understandings I came to. I hope we can get to some of my questions and some of yours." The vast majority of class time was inevitably spent on the questions that students had contributed.

Students as teachers and learners. Teachers not only expected to learn from students, some also expected students to learn from and teach each other. An underlying belief supporting this expectation was that students were competent and had valuable insights and experiences that could contribute to discussions within classroom environments.

This belief was enacted in several ways in the classrooms I observed. For example, Gloria continually encouraged students to talk with and teach each other through class formats that included small group discussions, group projects, and class discussions. In one case (12 April), she passed around a bag of quotations that she had generated from our readings and asked class participants to volunteer to describe what they had learned from or thought about particular quotations. In this way, students learned about others' interpretations of the texts, rather than only about their own or, perhaps, those held by Gloria.

Sarah also believed in the value of students' contributions. She expressed her valuing of students' ideas and a strategy that she used to encourage their participation:

> In [one] course I teach, I set it up exclusively so that they have to teach each other in a lot of different situations. Like I set the syllabus up so that not everyone reads the same thing, and they need to teach each other about things. All on the same topic or different perspectives on the same topic. One, because they can't possibly read everything they need to read professionally so this is a chance for them to learn from colleagues. But also because I think they get a lot out of talking about different perspectives and using somebody else's ideas with your ideas.

Sarah's words were put into practice in my observations of her class. She regularly asked students to work in small groups in order to encourage teaching and learning to and from each other. Additionally, Sarah often turned questions directed at her back to students, asking, "What do you think?" In doing this, she set up a classroom norm that established all participants as valuable contributors to each other's knowledge.

Andrea also believed that students' contributions to creating meaning and knowledge were important. In describing to me how she conveyed this belief to her students, she commented:

> I have studied this longer than you, but at the same time your experiences seem radically important to how you understand it. And also I believe that you have a lot to learn from your neighbor, that you might never even believe.

Finally, Rosa said one of her primary goals was trying "to set up a situation where [students] take each other seriously as producers of knowledge."

In my experience as a participant-observer in Mary Louise's class, the classroom environment was one that encouraged student teaching and learning. In my field notes, I wrote: "This evening was entertaining, moving, stimulating, intellectual, fun, and bonding. We all contributed tonight. We all have something valuable to contribute every night.'' These teachers believed that students had much to teach each other, and therefore tried to provide spaces in classroom discourse for student-to-student educational engagement to occur.

Teachers as teachers. Teachers spoke of their roles as encompassing not only learning from students, but also acting as teachers in a more traditional sense. Often teachers asserted that a very important role that they assumed was that of an experienced and studied participant in the knowledge presented or in the content area in which they taught. Rosa talked about her views:

> I think, for better or for worse, it's [the teacher's] knowledge that gets communicated to the students. And I'm not talking about the banking model, because I don't think that's the only thing, but finally I think that students want to know that you're going to teach them something. You have a certain kind of knowledge—a certain kind of authority based on your study—and your job is to communicate that. . . . I still believe in the absolute disciplinary nature of women's studies. . . . It's not just a method. It's not just a politics. It's material that one needs to know. So I think that it's a mistake to think that we aren't supposed to be giving them something that they can work with—an intellectual event, an experience.

Many teachers with whom I spoke planned for, and struggled to maintain, some degree of authority and acknowledged ''expertise'' as they fulfilled their roles as teachers in these classrooms.

Some of my observations bore this out as well. Kathy told her class on the second day that she would regularly be lecturing. Although she asked students to bring up points from the readings as well, she established that her predominant mode of teaching would establish her as presenting the most important knowledge on the topic to students. In another class, Ruth asked students to respond to a question, but then quickly put her own list of responses on an overhead for all to see. She then talked through her own list of ''answers,'' only infrequently responding to students' previous contributions.

Expansions of student and teacher roles. Students did not always easily accept attempts to encourage an expansion of the traditional roles of teachers and students in knowledge negotiation processes. As Susan Heald (1989) commented of her struggles,

> Students bring into our classes a host of pleasures, pains, and patterns around learning that are deeply ingrained as a result of [their] spending

most of their lives in school. I try to think of my teaching as about learning
how to think, but I find that this is not what students want to know. Many
want pieces of knowledge. (p. 22)

Teachers' experiences with students in this research occasionally reflected this occurrence. Some students wanted to hear from the presumed authority in the class—the teacher—rather than teach or learn
from each other. Several teachers commented on their struggles as they
attempted to get students to look at their peers as authority figures in
knowledge negotiations in these classes. Rosa presented her understanding of this dilemma:

It's just they're not very much trained to take each other seriously
as producers of knowledge. So it's hard to get them not to respond
to you and to respond to each other. They tend not to want to engage with each other for lots of different reasons. So beyond setting up artificial situations in which they have to do that, it's very
hard to get them to take each other seriously. That's a legacy, I
think, of our notion of meritocracy and individualism that just gets
brought into a feminist classroom and with which we all struggle.
And I think feminists struggle more because of this notion of collaborative learning and process.

Several teachers expressed their difficulty in trying to get students to
accept each other's experiences as valuable, even though the teachers
themselves recognized it as such.

Additionally, sometimes teachers were unsure where they should
step back from an "expert" role and encourage students to act as experts. Sometimes, students would not support the expansion of the
teaching role. As Chris told me,

You say things to students and they take it as the truth no matter
how much you talk about social construction. And we don't talk
about facts anymore . . . but they still accept it as facts and truth.
So that places a heavy burden on me as a faculty member, I feel, to
try and not misrepresent where things are.

In a way closely related to this, Vicki struggled with the delicate balance
needed to determine the most important pieces of information or conversations to have in a given classroom. For her, the hardest issue in her
teaching related to power and expertise in knowledge negotiations.
Vicki questioned, "How do you balance what they know against what I

know? What [do] they need to work through themselves versus what I have already figured out in some sense?" No clear answers for how to craft the most useful educational experiences possible were apparent.

Most teachers included in this research enacted practices that valued experiences and abilities from multiple sources. No one person in their classrooms ever totally decided how knowledge would be created and which processes would be most "effective" for which purposes. Although teachers and students continued to assume traditional roles in some ways, they often struggled to break out of the norms that dictated those roles.

Teachers and Students as Critical Thinkers or Challengers

> Society is not designed to educate people to remake it. Society is designed to educate people to maintain it.
>
> (Gloria, 26 April)

Several teachers believed that their roles encompassed challenging students' ideologies while simultaneously encouraging students to challenge themselves. With statements such as Gloria's, these teachers asked their students to examine how they and their meaning-making processes were constructed. They also encouraged students to examine the implications that those constructions might have. They wanted students to challenge their own ideologies as they grappled with course content and other ideological stances introduced into classroom discourse. Perhaps with an awareness of the situatedness of all ideological stances, several teachers questioned the multiple contextually embedded ideologies students brought to their classroom learning. Gloria explained how she tried to communicate her views to her class:

> When you say that someone is "to the right," they're to the right of you. Or to us. It's not like we're objective and we can stand out here and look at them. . . . While we're out here putting people on the continuum, we're somewhere too. And ideology is in relation to our ideology.

Rosa discussed her belief that it was important for students to challenge their own ideologies rather than to have a new ideology imposed on them by the teacher or class content:

> One can set up a classroom that will allow students to ask the questions so that it's not imposed. . . . If you pose the questions in the

right way or if you assign the right kinds of works, then the students are going to be more able to ask their own questions that lead you to the kind of productive discussions you might want to have as a feminist. . . . Merely bringing in a perspective from the outside isn't necessarily the way to go with introductory students.

Other teachers tried to get students to examine their own constructedness as it related to ways of thinking and, further, how it related to class content. Andrea said:

What I try to do is talk about [the topics] in a way that allows them entry into their own constructions. So that they can get curious about "You know I never thought about it like that before. I wonder how that has affected me or constructed me" and from there they can sort of like be thinking about their own [ideology] and what's happened to them.

Teachers often encouraged students to delve into their own ideologies and belief systems to examine how they were constructed and how they could attempt to construct themselves and their belief systems in the future.

Just as students were encouraged to question themselves and their own ideological positions, so too were they expected to examine and challenge positions represented by class content and content in the field in which that class was situated. Gloria talked about her views:

Everything we read, the first question is, "What's the underlying ideological position?" It's not "just true." The person is somewhere, has some perspective, believes something. . . . The person who wrote this has some theoretical notion of why things work the way they do.

Some teachers acknowledged that challenging one's own ideologies was not an easy process, especially when related to the often personal and controversial nature of the class content. Julie discussed her understanding of this difficulty:

Even students who probably aren't aware of how they might be engaging with [class content], there's some real fundamental questions that we ask that, if they're not too busy resisting, often do have an impact. It's uncomfortable. We deal with really uncomfortable topics in this course. . . . It's hard for people.

Kathy talked about how the topics in her class proved challenging to students as well:

> We talk about how racism and race and gender and class are really loaded issues right now and that there is really no way of discussing this without being aware of the fact that you're going to be emotional about it. There are no distinctions between this intellectual high ground that we take [and] the emotional aspects of this stuff.

In one attempt to alleviate some of the personal difficulty that accompanies discussions of these controversial topics, Gloria wrote on her syllabus, "Ideas, not individuals, are open to challenge." Though perhaps, at times, this is a difficult distinction, Gloria felt it useful to delineate between the concepts that were being challenged and the people who were embracing those concepts. Class content was a particular challenge as students acknowledged, engaged with, and, sometimes, modified their own assumptions and ideologies.

Mary Louise also realized that a challenging or critical approach to class content was often difficult for students who were not used to examining the underlying assumptions of a given piece of work with which they were asked to engage. She posed the difficulty in this way:

> I guess that is one of my goals—that people are taking on different positions, looking from different positions at the work. It's very hard to do. . . . It seems alien. . . . [We] live out our experiences. And those experiences don't foster taking multiple positions and interrogating.

By asking the class, "Can you interrupt the meanings other people have made?" (25 April), Mary Louise stressed that students needed to think critically about classroom texts. Several teachers discussed the examination of contemporary ideologies and ways of thinking as an important aspect of teaching and learning in their classrooms.

While many teachers were aware of the difficulty of reexamining one's ideological frameworks, a student in Gloria's class described how she experienced Gloria's method of challenging the students:

> Gloria plants seeds. She has a way of getting into every crack and corner of your thinking, exposing all those old and rusty ideas that have for so long limited vision and inhibited action. I think the real impact of the class is yet to come for me. I have taken away so

much, and can only wonder at what all I have missed. I am so
thankful to have had the opportunity to sit under her teaching.

Depending on the ways in which a challenge is perceived, students can
have multiple and varied reactions.

What is the expected outcome from this examining? Several teachers commented on what they hoped would happen through this approach. Sarah told me:

> One of the things that I also try to do is to get them to deconstruct
> a lot of their own beliefs so that they can remain open to a new way
> of looking at things. . . . What I try to do is get them to take apart
> all these assumptions about why this is a practice and to look at cer-
> tain cultural norms and who benefits.

And Kathy spoke of her intentions:

> The basic point is trying to get people to understand that there are
> various ways of understanding the world. And one of them is by
> dislocating yourself from privilege in whichever way you want to
> say. And another is by questioning the notion of identity and natu-
> ralness and normalness.

Another teacher expressed what she perceived to be the optimal outcome of students' questioning their own stances on given topics. In
Mary Louise's words, "I think the best that would happen is that people
get to think of other ways to look at things. I guess the best thing that
would happen is they better respect and understand the role of [oth-
ers]." And Julie talked about reactions that she has had from students
that suggested the degree to which her class affected students' ways of
thinking. She said, "I literally know that a lot of people end up thinking
of things in a way that will never be the same."

Several teachers, however, believed that involvement in their
classes did not always change the ways in which people think. One
teacher expressed her disappointment when asked how she felt about
those students who refused to challenge their own ways of thinking.
Referring to a specific situation, Kathy said:

> It's not okay [if students don't examine their thinking] because . . .
> how they think and feel and act has real implications for the next
> generation of the so called others. It makes me feel two ways. One
> is disappointed that it never really got any further than that. And

that they really had the privilege of shaking us all in a way that White women or gay men or others in the course don't. But on the other hand, I feel like at least in the back of their minds, they will always have this other discourse running. And that if I'm lucky, at some crucial point, . . . they will at least be informed somehow.

Teachers reported varying degrees of success at getting people to engage with and challenge their own ideologies and those represented by others in the class or in class content.

A few teachers told me that they conceptualized this challenging aspect of their roles somewhat differently. They believed that they themselves needed to be challenged and have their ideologies "exposed" when working with students. Rae discussed how she did this in her class:

[We] talk about just noticing how we respond internally to people who are different from us. And [we] do it with some compassion for ourselves. To think, Where did that idea come from? Is it one I still want to hang on to? If not, I know I'm going to have to work for a long time because it's in there.

Rae fully incorporated herself in the process of crafting classroom challenges to ideologies and assumptions.

Other teachers expressed their own personal discomfort in challenging students, depending on the particular classroom context. As Cheryl put it,

bell hooks . . . talks about pedagogy in ways that she tries to confront students. . . . And she talks about students in her classroom and their anger. And she says this is fine because learning isn't supposed to be comfortable. I agree with that to a certain extent, but I also think that clearly says to me that she is exercising authority in the classroom if she is trying to encourage students' anger through confrontation. And I don't think that's quite the answer for me either.

Confrontation can take on different meanings and possibilities for teaching and learning depending on practices that affect and are contested in particular classrooms.

What, then, are participants' intents, values, norms, and customs in the ways in which they view the process of knowledge production and negotiation? Customs expressed by many teachers in my study

valued critical thought and understandings of content as related to ideological positions. Classroom norms problematized both classroom work
and the belief structures that supported that work. In some cases, students' previous educational experiences supported this critical experience. In other cases, students questioned the value of such an approach.
Additionally, to varying degrees, teachers and students in this feminist
teaching discourse both examined their own positionalities, and considered how "where they were coming from" affected their abilities and
desires to engage in certain types of knowledge negotiations. This valuing of a constant self-examination supported knowledge negotiation
processes that were flexible, changing, critical, and, many times, difficult.

Teachers as Classroom Managers

A further custom that teachers discussed in my research was that
which placed them in the role of classroom manager. Closely related to
the role of teacher as monitor, most teachers expressed in interviews
that they were comfortable performing this role as they constructed it.
In managing classroom experiences, teachers expected student involvement in classroom knowledge negotiations in a variety of ways—
through journal writing, participation in class discussions, attendance
at class meetings, or other outside assignments. Tonika discussed how,
in one of her smaller classes, she established certain guidelines for participation at the beginning of the course:

> We had certain rules that I set up at the very beginning of the se-
> mester. One is that this is a small class and as a small class, every-
> body is committed to the course. And being committed to the class
> means . . . that you're going to be here every time we meet. You
> are going to be here. . . . You have to be here. You have to take
> part [in] each class. You have to be part of the discussion in each
> class.

Rae set up guidelines for class structuring as well. She felt, however,
that doing so with students was more useful than doing so alone, as a
joint effort would allow all classroom participants to feel a sense of
responsibility for managing classroom discourse.

Another aspect of managing classroom discourse that teachers often performed was as discussion or dialogue facilitators. They held
themselves responsible for keeping the dialogue open and the discus-

sion going. Mary Louise explained her view of this responsibility and
how she structured her classroom so that she could fulfill it:

> Sometimes when something is really hard to read, usually in my
> graduate class, I ask someone to go to the board and write down
> the questions that come up. In part, I do it because I want to be
> able to negotiate all the voices participating in the discussion. . . .
> It's better if somebody else does it so I can keep the conversation
> going.

Keeping the discussion going and providing opportunities for dialogue
and participation in class also related to the degree to which teachers
could maintain an environment in which students could feel safe.

Creating and maintaining classrooms as safe spaces within which
ideas could be troubled was a further custom or role that many teachers
discussed with me. They felt that it was an important part of their role
in knowledge negotiation processes to ensure that students felt as safe
as possible in that environment to test uncertain ideas and views. Mary
Louise expressed her conviction:

> I want people to be very engaged in what we're doing. I want to
> make it a very enjoyable experience. I want them to be able to ques-
> tion each other in a way that's not hurtful. I've talked a lot to stu-
> dents who've said that they feel safe to speak in class, and in other
> classes they've taken, it doesn't feel safe. Having one's ideas re-
> spected is very important in my teaching. . . . What I try to create
> is the sense that I'm co-responsible with the people in the class
> [for] their learning. I mean, if they're not learning, it's not, you
> know, all their responsibility. I have to provide an environment
> where together we can trouble ideas.

Working to manage and create an environment as conducive as possible
to all classroom participants was a goal of many in feminist teaching
discourse. Yet, as will be discussed in chapter 8, the desire both for
"freedom of speech" and for classroom safety often created tensions for
these classroom managers.

While an understanding of teachers as classroom managers certainly applied in many situations, my observations led me to understand how this concept was expanded in a few cases. In Sarah's class,
when a student asked if she was talking too much, Sarah responded
with, "We'll tell you." By including other students in her statement,

she supported the idea that students have both the responsibility and the authority to shape their classroom environments. In another case, Gloria (10 May) said that she was going to have to start "cracking the whip" and keeping student presentations within their allotted time. For the entire class, however, she chose not to enforce the time limit even once.

The environment that I felt most clearly evinced the element of co-responsibility for managing classroom discourses was that of Mary Louise's class. On a day when students were to present written work to each other, she asked the class how they wanted to proceed (28 February). She suggested that they break into smaller groups, if this was acceptable to others in the class, because "I'm just not mean enough to cut people off. . . . It feels awful to say you have to stop." Additionally, Mary Louise sometimes asked how the class wanted to proceed, whether staying together or breaking up into smaller groups. She also remained silent at times, so that other class participants could determine the next course of action. This shared responsibility for managing the classroom was demonstrated clearly on one occasion when a student was interrupted and was unable to finish verbalizing his thought. Shortly thereafter, another student, rather than Mary Louise, asked that they listen to what the previous student had wanted to say. Nevertheless, even in this environment, students recognized that Mary Louise, as the teacher, did retain some control over their environment. In the words of one student (21 March), "What you [Mary Louise] said the other day—that you're really in charge because you picked the texts— that's true. If you had picked different texts, we'd be having a different conversation."

The practices that were espoused in these feminist classrooms demonstrated the sometimes contradictory values of a feminist teaching discourse. Many teachers valued safety, and yet simultaneously wanted contested discourse. Subsequently, knowledge that was validated through these negotiation processes was that which could be expressed, created, and constructed through environments that were both non-threatening and respectful, and also difficult and challenging.

Teachers and Students as Knowledge Contributors

Perhaps the practice that feminist educators in this research most often discussed and problematized in conversations and observations was the use of "experience" in knowledge negotiations within their classrooms. While I focused earlier on *how* teachers sought to be responsive to students and their experiences, here I concentrate on various ways in which experience was called upon in knowledge negotiations in feminist classrooms.

Many scholars have examined the use of experience in formal educational environments (Heald, 1989; Lewis, 1993; Middleton, 1993; Swartzlander, Pace, & Stamler, 1993; Weedon, 1987). Others have argued that the separation between academic and experiential knowledge sets up a hierarchy of "acceptable" or "most valuable" knowledge that excludes certain types of relational knowing (Heald, 1989). As Parker Palmer (1983) commented, "Conventional education strives not to locate and understand the self in the world, but to get it out of the way" (p. 35). Yet Chris Weedon (1987) believed that "the meaning of experience is perhaps the most crucial site of political struggle over meaning since it involves personal, psychic and emotional investment on the part of the individual" (p. 79). And Sue Middleton (1993) felt that "we must devise ways of teaching students about the various feminist perspectives in ways that focus them on students' everyday personal, intellectual, and political dilemmas" (p. 31). The use of experience has certainly been a contested site for knowledge production and negotiations.

Teachers included in this research spoke as well about the uses of experience in knowledge construction. Vicki talked about her methods:

> I use experience and the issue of experience in all my classes from "intro." to advanced graduate classes, but I use it differently in different classes and depending in many cases on the size of the class. When I taught the large . . . course, for one portion of the class we had students . . . write a journal. We invited the students to be connecting their personal experience to what they are reading . . . to see what is imbedded in [a] story, how it relates to them. . . . In other words, getting them to think of education not as something abstract and divorced from the rest of one's life, but thoroughly integrated with it.

Sharon also believed that experiential knowledge is sometimes educationally useful: "There are moments when I think personal experience is extremely relevant. And there are others when I think it is not." In Sharon's case, she herself decided what types of experience were relevant or "on track" for the classroom knowledge negotiations. Perhaps this was because of her concern that "if you use experience and self-disclosure there is no question that you run the risk of making the class seem less academic."

Recently, several scholars have problematized an absence of teachers' experiences from classroom discourse. For example, Kathleen Rockhill (1993) said, "Although I do not want to impose my emotion, I cannot expect students to enter into the vulnerable place of expressing their feelings if I stay safely masked, hiding behind the role of teacher" (p. 355). Simultaneously, however, others have problematized the use of teachers' "personal" experiences in classroom settings. Madeleine Grumet (1991) has pointed out the difficult assumptions and negative aspects that inform the use of personal experience or knowledge:

> Personal knowledge in this scheme is constituted by the stories about experience we usually keep to ourselves, and practical knowledge by the stories that are never, or rarely, related, but provide, nevertheless, the structure for the improvisations that we call coping, problem solving, action. The politics of personal knowledge demand that we acknowledge that telling is an alienation, that telling diminishes the teller, and that we who invite teachers to tell us their stories develop an ethic for that work. (p. 70)

With Rockhill, Grumet recognizes the dangerous possibilities in unquestioningly using students' or teachers' personal knowledges or experiences as class material.

Another difficulty in the use of experience in these settings is the evaluative custom in which students and teachers engage with each other. This custom is problematized by the question, What relationship should the use of (or exposure of) personal experience in formal classroom settings have to evaluation in that setting? Harland Bloland (1995) proposed that

> in a postmodern era, there is danger of the collapse of the distinction between knowledge inside the academy and outside of it, with the result that certain kinds of knowledge that used to be the monopoly of the academy are now shared with institutions outside of the academy. (p. 537)

When previous knowledge distinctions become obscured, must not the evaluation function of classroom experience and teaching be reformed as well? Susan Heald (1989) was in a quandary with this seeming mismatch:

> Having asked students to accept the relationship between their academic work and their lives, they must then trust us with the results. Inevitably, we are going to assign them a mark for their efforts, and marking papers like this comes to be very much like a judgement on people's lives. (p. 25)

Is a higher education grade to be a judgment on the use of people's lives or on the material that is dictated by the teacher? If we reestablish teachers' authority to solely dictate what constitutes "important" classroom knowledge, does that then throw us back to a time when classroom content and knowledge negotiations were only tangentially related to students' lives and lived experiences? Is the use of personal knowledge in formal classrooms an invasive prying into areas that students may not want to reveal? While experiential knowledge continued to be valued in various ways among the teachers with whom I spoke, they simultaneously recognized the dangers of using both their own and students' experience in formal education.

EMERGING PRACTICES AND CRITIQUES OF KNOWLEDGE

> Common-sense knowledge is not a monolithic, fixed body of knowledge. It is often contradictory and subject to change. It is not always necessarily conservative in its implications. Its political effects depend on the particular context in which it is articulated. However, its power comes from its claim to be natural, obvious and therefore true. It looks to "human nature" to guarantee its version of reality. It is the medium through which already fixed "truths" about the world, society and individuals are expressed.
>
> (Weedon, 1987, p. 77)

In this chapter, I have contemplated beliefs and practices that influenced knowledge construction and negotiation within these classrooms. I further questioned commonsense knowledge of teaching and learning. I turn now to the customs and critiques that these texts, when juxtaposed with poststructuralism, seem to suggest for future poststructural feminist teaching discourses.

First, through this research I learned that knowledge negotiations in a poststructural feminist teaching discourse are tentative and transitional. In other words, the actions and beliefs that support and inform feminist teaching practice must be continually reevaluated and questioned, both by feminist teachers and critical others, in order to examine their potential use. In Eileen's words,

> [Teaching is] like trying out strategies and reproducing some loud experiment that you hope will have a certain kind of result. So I think that unreliably . . . you can try certain kinds of things that had some effect in the past as long as you are always provisional about them and always seeing that the circumstances are changing. . . . I think that really, the first thing is always understanding that what it's going to produce is changing.

Factors such as content, students, and the many unknowable aspects of our own and others' lives that affect classroom dynamics in multiple ways call for an approach to negotiating knowledge that is tentative and provisional. Classrooms, in feminist poststructural teaching discourse, would be question based, rather than answer based. Knowledge negotiations would be fluid and dynamic. Stages or processes could not be guaranteed.

Second, a poststructural feminist teaching practice calls for a critical expansion of traditional knowledge in formal classroom knowledge negotiations. With this expansion or redefinition comes an understanding that what is traditionally understood to be "formal" or "academic" knowledge was produced with certain motivations and intentions. Ideologies become a site of contestation and interrogation. As Sue Middleton (1993) said, "If students are to understand feminist educational theories, it is important that they understand the educational conditions and wider social circumstances of their production" (p. 29). She commented further that institutional structures of knowledge tend to limit the usefulness of knowledge construction. In Middleton's words, "I could never fit my ideas about educational theory into the disciplinary categories that formed its institutionalized basis. . . . The hierarchies of academic and professional knowledge—the fences around territories—fragment and divide us" (p. 172). In relation to poststructuralism, Harland Bloland (1995) contended that "[higher education] cannot act as though it spoke truths; it can argue only that what it does is useful, but not that it is true" (p. 551). Ideologies and presumed truths, through feminist poststructural discourse, must be examined for use-value, rather than truth-value.

Closely related to this critical expansion of traditional ideas, a poststructural feminist teaching discourse struggles to understand the contextual embeddedness both of educational processes and of individual student and teacher lives. In Mary Louise's reflections on her own teaching, she wrote:

> Through the course, I hoped to heighten teachers' attention to literacy teaching and learning not only as activities . . . on which so much emphasis is placed in schools, teacher education, and in the assessment of individuals, but also as ways in which people make, negotiate, and contest meanings among others, across time, and in various places. (Gomez, in press)

Several teachers in this study discussed the ways in which their practices were situated within a larger environment that had tremendous impacts on teaching and learning.

A poststructural feminist teaching discourse remains open to continual examination of the underlying themes that inform classroom knowledge negotiations. Therefore, the ideas that I propose here become, like other knowledge, situational and limited the moment they are placed on paper. The use of these conceptualizations of a poststructural feminist teaching discourse serves as a (hopefully) provocative entry into the application of feminist poststructural approaches and questions into higher education classrooms.

CHAPTER 7

Classroom Ruptures:
Politics of Difference

Each individual derives varying amounts of penalty and privilege from the multiple systems of oppression which frame everyone's lives.

(Collins, 1991, p. 229)

Diversity and *difference* are terms that scholars have often discussed in contemporary reflections about teaching and learning in higher education environments (hooks, 1994; H. Giroux, 1993). They take on a variety of meanings, all of which have their advocates and opponents. Establishing customs of "dealing with" or "celebrating" difference in our society is certainly contested terrain.

The discourse of feminist teaching does not exist outside of that contestation. Indeed, many feminist scholars and teachers have reflected on their own practices and beliefs in relation to difference. Marilyn Frye (1992a) asserted,

> We have had great difficulty coming to terms with the fact of differences among women—differences associated with race, class, ethnicity, religion, nationality, sexuality, age, physical ability and even such variety among women as is associated just with peculiarities of individual personal history. (p. 62)

Frances Maher and Mary Kay Thompson Tetreault (1994) stressed that "position, perhaps more than any other single factor, influences the construction of knowledge, and . . . positional factors reflect relationships of power both within and outside the classroom itself" (p. 22). However, they wrote,

> the meanings people create about aspects of themselves, like gender, cultural identification, and class position, vary widely in different classrooms.

116

> Although these meanings are in constant flux, they nevertheless reflect the unequal power relations that govern the society outside the classroom. (p. 202)

bell hooks (1994) also believed that respecting, and working among and for, differences and diversity has been a difficult task for feminist or liberatory educators:

> Many folks found that as they tried to respect "cultural diversity" they had to confront the limitations of their training and knowledge, as well as a possible loss of "authority." Indeed, exposing certain truths and biases in the classroom often created chaos and confusion. The idea that the classroom should always be a "safe," harmonious place was challenged. It was hard for individuals to fully grasp the idea that recognition of difference might also require of us a willingness to see the classroom change, to allow for shifts in relations between students. (p. 30)

This attention to difference, which has the potential to disrupt what are understood to be normal and safe educational environments, took many different forms.

Much feminist work has struggled with concepts of difference, especially in terms of developing understandings within the category of women. As Marilyn Frye (1992a) wrote,

> No one encounters the world simply as *a woman*. Nobody observes and theorizes simply as *a woman*. If there are in every locale perspectives and meaning which can properly be called women's, there is nonetheless no such thing as *a* or *the* woman's story of what is going on. (p. 62)

Magda Gere Lewis (1993) suggested that although it is impossible to identify a common experience among all persons of a given group, it is nevertheless crucial to examine broad social expectations and understandings of certain characteristics that enable some persons to walk in the world differently than others. As Lewis described it,

> While it is important not to reduce every particular individual to the collective of which they happen to be a part, at the same time, however, we cannot shrink away from uncovering those forms of social relations that mark and brutalize, both individually and collectively, those who carry the weighted baggage of their gender, class, race, and sexual desires—forms that continue to perpetuate oppressive and hurtful experiences. (p. 13)

Both Frye and Lewis urge feminists to continue the difficult struggle of understanding, celebrating, and benefitting from differences found in their communities.

A focus on difference within feminist classrooms may be difficult; however, critical concepts in both feminism and poststructuralism provoke its examination. Feminist approaches that focus on equality between persons of oppressed and oppressor groups have suggested grave outcomes if current differences and inequities are not addressed in classrooms. Poststructural approaches conceptualize difference and equality as being politically and socially problematic. The differences inherent in both those who form and those who are served by contradictory higher education institutions must be taken into account by those both within and outside their gates.

Poststructural thinkers have paid much attention to the ways in which multiple and contested approaches to difference inform our understandings of higher education (Carlson, 1995; Lather, 1991). Differences, in poststructural thought, are not binary. In other words, while we may be constructed as having only two options for being, that construction can be expanded to encompass multiple options that are included between and beyond what are seen as polar opposites. Poststructural approaches propose that differences are constructed by complex and continual interactions that occur between languages, knowledges, and power constructions of diverse groups.

In this chapter, I consider the ways in which differences were approached, understood, and constructed by teachers who participated in my research by asking, How does power affect and relate to the expression of difference? I respond to this question by addressing first a desire for commonality, and then differences in identities, beliefs, and learning styles or approaches. I discuss tensions that teachers experienced in their evolving understandings of difference, as well as in their attempts to implement these understandings. Finally, I conclude this chapter with thoughts on possibilities for difference as constructed within a feminist poststructural teaching discourse.

DESIRE FOR COMMONALITY

Several teachers in this study wanted students to recognize their commonalities as well as their differences in learning and interacting with each other. This desire for commonality was not to diminish differences, but rather was for the purpose of creating a foundation of openness and mutual respect so that differences could subsequently be explored through class material and discussion. As Gloria told me, "People's personhood is important. It doesn't matter what their race, class, gender, sexuality is. Their personhood is important. They are not less of a person because they're White, middle class and heterosexual. They're people, too." Closely related to this, Deborah described her beliefs:

> There is a fear that the more you study single groups, the more the United States will be balkanized. I don't feel I'm working to tear apart the fabric of the United States. I'm working toward a kind of healing. I want people to find themselves and get closer to their own identities and their own pasts and their own families. It's a good thing in that the more everyone can find out what other people's histories and stories [are], the closer we'll all be. This knowledge is not pulling us apart, it's bringing us together.

She explained further:

> We're all alike because we're all human beings, but we're not all alike because we come from different cultural backgrounds. And so, if we don't know anything about those other cultures, then we should read these books because those markers are interesting. They're interesting because it expands our own palette to taste different kinds of foods. It expands our own knowledge of the world to have other languages. And so those differences can enrich our life experience. All people can have an underlying similarity, but the differences are also important because they are what identify us.

Kathy's views were similar. She described to me how she encouraged her classes to look at both difference and sameness:

> I get them to see that we're talking about probably 2% difference and 98% sameness. I explain to them that in the European scholarly tradition, people went in looking to define difference. But if we sort of explode that whole way of thinking and sort of go in and look at sameness and difference, we see this overwhelming sameness that really should cause us to pay heed to how we construct difference, because you put a lot of emphasis on something that is very, very small. . . . And don't get me wrong. I'm not arguing any of the universality. I'm not arguing any sort of 100% humanity as a lot of people do, to sort of belie the whole question of identity and power and how power gets played out. That's not it at all. I'm simply asking people to reconceptualize difference, first of all, so we can go on and talk about how this thing called difference,

which may not be all that great, gets blown into this huge thing in [a] playing out of power.

Kathy, Deborah, and Gloria believed that developing commonality and, perhaps, community as a base for class interaction and eventually exploring difference was a useful practice. Interestingly, this desire for commonality was proposed most clearly by three women of color.

An approach to differences through commonality, though, was not the practice that all teachers chose to adopt. In her class, Julie struggled to figure out "how you validate experiences without assuming anything is a common experience." She assumed that it was either not useful or not possible to establish commonality among class members. She, like others, chose to focus almost exclusively on difference.

DIFFERENCE AND IDENTITIES

One type of difference that most of the teachers in this study described as affecting their teaching practices was that which related to identities. Whereas previously I focused on teachers' individual identities, here I discuss the concepts related to identity differences largely as they intersected with class material and students. Sometimes, an attention to identity differences took the form of discussing one particular aspect of identity (such as race, class, gender, ability, religion, and sexuality). More often, though, teachers asserted in their words and actions that identities were multifaceted composites made up of a variety of characteristics and cultural beliefs. In this section, I touch briefly on race as a singular aspect of identity because of its overwhelming presence in discussions of difference in this research. I then focus on a multifaceted understanding of identity and teachers' implementations of their beliefs in relation to this understanding.

Several teachers included in this research believed that racial constructions of difference affected their teaching practices. Andrea described how students in her class struggled with race more than gender:

The big leap for most Wisconsin White women is race . . . is Whiteness. It's not that big a leap for them to get the gender problematics. It's a big leap for them to get some kind of consciousness about what it might mean to be White and how that affects gender and class.

Andrea then described how she approached this topic in class:

> I talk about how Whiteness is so normalized that we don't think about it. And we do [think about] gender because it's a way that we can interact in the world, but White isn't. So that there's a sense that if you're a White person you've kind of been normalized in such a way that you don't think about it.

Similarly, Kathy told me she emphasized to her students that "what we're doing [in the classroom] is not situating Whiteness and whatever else as the normalness, at the center, and then looking out and then calling that difference." Andrea and Kathy emphasized to White students in their classes that it would be helpful to look at the ways they were "inside" the socially defined "normal" and what that meant for their understandings of others and racial difference.

Sharon discussed how race affected her classroom teaching as well. She described to me her discomfort in teaching a class that used texts written by Black women when there were few Black women in the class:

> I was anxious. Not because I was dealing with Black women writers, which I had done regularly, but because of the composition of the class. It was very, very difficult. And I worried about it every day. The whole semester was horrible because I did so much worrying. But it never really got resolved. No awful thing happened, and it may have been a reasonably good class, and I think we learned a lot. But there was a tension all the time and it was [because of] the fear of offending someone.

Another teacher highlighted race as a central concept of difference in her teaching as well. Vicki described to me that those who are visibly different in some way from the majority were more likely to discuss those differences in class. Most often, this visible difference related to race. As she said,

> Women who are racially different from the majority of the class are more likely to allude to it and make it relevant to what they say than, for example, lesbian women. . . . If your difference is not visibly evident and you have to make a decision whether or not to disclose, I think there is less free allusion to one's difference [than] when the difference is visible. . . . So I think there are interesting

differences in student self-disclosure depending on what kind of difference a woman feels she has.

Finally, Deborah conveyed some difficulties that she had in her classes when students believed that differences between persons of varying races were so great that they could not derive any benefit from reading or struggling with works describing or based in cultures other than their own. Deborah told me of one incident:

> [A White student] felt that she couldn't relate to [a text written by a person from a culture other than the student's own]—there was no way she could relate to it. I tried to be very patient, but at one point I just lost my cool and I said, "What about relating to it as a human being?" She was writing about them to me as though [members of that culture were] baboons or something—as though she's a human being and they're not. I was very offended and I got angry. I said, "What is this? Why can't you relate to this? They're human beings. You're a human being. You must get underneath that and not let those superficial differences get in the way."

Sharon, Vicki, and Deborah, with several others, believed that racial identity affected not only broad social understandings and structures, but also understandings that were forming within their classrooms.

At the same time, I learned that most teachers in this research saw difference as a complex and tentative concept that went beyond racial boundaries. Tonika told me that she sees identity as an intersection of a variety of characteristics. She described her resulting teaching approaches:

> I don't teach a course in which I say the topic of the course today is gender or the topic of the course today is race. . . . Three issues are essentially continually being dealt with over and over and over in just about all the material that I teach in classes. And I try to use them in a way in which they are not separable from each other. They are interdependent. The outcome is always because of the interdependence of the events. They hang largely on race, class, and gender.

Alex supported this approach, but said that her students sometimes didn't understand her expanded notion of difference: "They think when you talk about diversity or multiculturalism, that you are talking about ethnicity. And that issues related to age, disability, gender, sexual orientation are not multicultural issues. They might be something else, but they're not multicultural." And Gloria said, "When these two things [race and gender] come together they make something even different. It isn't just about gender or it isn't just about class [or just] about race."

Teachers approached these identity differences in many ways. Rae described how she incorporated multiple identity positions into her classroom:

> One of the things that I feel best about is the way I have integrated the notion of difference into all the classes. . . . I do sessions that are focused on multiculturalism but those issues get woven into the readings all along with guests that we invite in. Like, for example, [students] see more gays and lesbians then they will ever know they've seen.

And while not yet proposing a strategy to accomplish what she saw as a thorough integration of differences, Andrea believed that

> that would be the crux of being the most excellent feminist teacher in my mind—if the students have a sense that they would be interacting with the issues no matter what they were—sexuality, race, class, body size, beauty, ability, all those things—so that people in the class don't get erased.

Difference in identity characteristics was seen by most of the teachers in this research as a complex and tentative concept informed by many sources.

DIFFERENCE AND BELIEFS

Another type of difference that served as a source of tension for some of the teachers in this research related to different or conflicting beliefs presented by classroom participants or texts. Teachers often hoped that the understandings and convictions developed or resisted in their classes could inform students' actions outside of class, preferably in ways that would create greater equity. Simultaneously, teachers wanted to allow for a wide variety of views within their classroom environments. At times, these two beliefs conflicted with each other and the resulting tension was difficult to rectify.

In an interview, I asked Mary Louise about a specific situation in which students were resisting views which, she believed, were based on equity principles. I asked how she felt knowing that these students didn't change their beliefs during the class. Her response was as follows:

> It was hard for me. I think what I came to think in the end is that it is OK. I mean, OK in the sense that I only teach them for a semester. I have to be respectful of the beliefs that they come to teaching with. So that's OK. And I want to provide a forum where it's safe for them to say what they think. . . . In one sense, it's OK. In another sense, it's not OK. I'm afraid about the kind of practices that these young people will engage in regardless of whether it's conservative Christian or all-White suburban school or anything else—[they] will not respect the differences among people, differences that are culturally based or grounded in one's socioeconomic positioning. . . . I think of the questions that I ask about race and sexual orientation, in terms of how to be respectful with all pupils and with teachers. Those [students] are the people who need to ask themselves these questions—students who are [from] well-off, conservative suburban communities. . . . [They] always need to ask themselves questions about how they're serving students.

Mary Louise commented in a subsequent interview:

> I'm always wondering, how far do I push? You know, before that person is distressed and will shut off his or her thinking. So it's something that I attend to a great deal as a teacher. And it's uncomfortable not necessarily in a bad way, but it makes me—it's tension for me. How much do I question? How much do I make clear what I'm thinking because I want the person to engage with the ideas? I'm not out to change the way they think, but rather to say, "Here's some alternative dimensions to play around with in terms of your concerns."

From Mary Louise and several other teachers in this research, I learned that determining how strongly to encourage students to rethink their views was a difficult decision.

Some teachers in this study described how they appreciated and encouraged a wide variety of views in their classes, thereby diminishing the belief that there was an "answer" or a "truth." For example, although the course content in Brianne's class explicitly focused on feminism, she tried to keep her class discussion open for a wide variety of interpretations of feminism. In another situation, Vicki told me:

> Even in a lecture format, I try to validate the notion that there is no single approach that is right, that there are quite a number of legitimate positions and let's think about each of them. What are the strengths and weaknesses? And I ask the students to see where they are.

Kelly told me about her perspectives on different beliefs, even when those differences seem to be contradictory. In her words,

> One thing I value I guess is contradictions. Contradictions in terms of what's going on in the text. But I should say that contradictions are valued because contradiction can often open up a kind of struggle or tension. And I think that the contradictions, struggles, and tensions are often the source of some sort of change. . . . I'll often underscore that and by the same token often when I sort of presented students with a reading or a text, I will present them with different and often opposing interpretations.

In an observation of Sarah's class, I saw her enact a strategy to incorporate many differing views as well. When asked to report back on a particularly challenging small group meeting in which I participated, students at first didn't respond. Finally, one group member said that they probably don't have a spokesperson because they all have different views. Sarah responded by saying, "Well, then let's hear lots."

Gloria implemented a teaching strategy that allowed for and encouraged differing beliefs and perspectives and yet did not force students to speak in class if they were uncomfortable, or to "own" their contradictory statements. She asked students to respond to a question that she had posed by writing on large index cards that she had provided. After several minutes, Gloria collected the cards that students had responded on. As she was getting ready to read the cards aloud to the class, she said, "Please don't feel any compulsion to defend what you think is yours. These are now a collective—they are ours." She then proceeded to read all of the cards while people listened to each others' words and perspectives. In this way, different views and understandings were expressed; yet the environment was made as "safe" as possible for students because they were not forced to claim or defend their questions or beliefs.

In a discussion, Jasmine expressed that she had often heard teachers in women's studies criticized for "indoctrinating" their students, and not allowing different beliefs to be expressed. She told me about her frustration and disbelief in those criticisms and said,

> I think indoctrination by definition is not feminist teaching. Yes, I would like it if my students would leave my class being antiracist. But I help by discussing the issues, really talking about it, and maybe they will be able to get to that point, you know, without being brainwashed or whatever [critics] think is going on. I think there are students who are fairly susceptible to charismatic teachers in anything. That's why people choose to go into the field they are in. They decide to go into English because they had a charismatic English teacher. So we don't think of that as indoctrination into English. So the students get excited about feminism because there is this dynamic, exciting teacher. What does that get interpreted as? Indoctrination. I would say that I've never seen indoctrination. I've seen teachers who have been maybe not as flexible in hearing some students who come from a very antifeminist point of view, but on the other hand, you can get irritated by students who come from any inflexible point of view.

Most teachers included in this research felt strongly that they did not want to indoctrinate their students or force them to change their belief systems. Rather, they hoped that through examination of the material presented and participation in discussions, students would understand and be aware of other options or ways of thinking that were available to them. As discussed in chapter 6, a few teachers expressed the desire to be reflexive of their own ideologies as well.

DIFFERENCE AND LEARNING STYLES

Another type of difference that teachers addressed during this research was the difference in students' preferred learning styles. In smaller classes, particularly, teachers would try to adapt classrooms to fit a wide variety of learning preferences. For example, Gloria provided students with multiple evaluation options from which they could choose so that they could excel in ways with which they were comfortable:

> I think what I've learned about these evaluation options is partly . . . that everybody can be excellent in this class, but you have to

give a little room to demonstrate that. You can't say everybody's got to toe dance. Some people will not be able to get up on their toes. But instead, I say there's a lot of dancin' goin' on here, and here are the different ways.

The teachers in this study provided me with many examples of the ways in which they attempted to incorporate a diversity of learning styles. Although it is difficult to fully capture teachers' myriad approaches here, I will discuss some of the strategies that they used to accommodate students' multiple learning preferences.

While I was observing her classroom, Sarah wrote a question on the board about a central topic in their course and told students that she hadn't given her answer to this on purpose because she thought that there were many different answers, and she wanted to allow those multiple views to come out. She asked that people first ponder the question, then look at the readings for that day's class while considering their responses to the question. They were to then have an ongoing conversation on the board—writing and pushing their own and others' comments and thoughts. Sarah also told students that their responses didn't have to be in the form of words, but could also be pictures or songs.

Gloria and Mary Louise provided multiple ways of learning and participating in their classrooms. For example, Gloria asked students to write research proposals, essays, pedagogical journals, participate in large and small group discussions, and read a wide variety of both required and optional texts. In addition, she brought in videos and popular press material. Mary Louise asked students to write about their literacy development or a story about their teaching. She asked for a final paper, the topic of which was entirely defined by students. And, too, she provided opportunities for both large and small group discussion that was based on students' questions. By providing these multiple sources for students to interact with the various texts of classroom discourses, these feminist teachers attempted to accommodate and support difference in light of students' various learning styles.

EMERGING PRACTICES AND CRITIQUES OF DIFFERENCE

In this chapter I have discussed the educational deliberations about difference by the teachers in my study. I have both provided strategies for and described difficulties of teaching and learning within and about various forms of difference. I turn now to what I am learning about norms and possibilities of and for poststructural feminist teaching discourse as well as its approaches to difference in higher education settings.

First, in feminist poststructural teaching discourse there is a recognition of difficulties in educating about differences, especially as each participant embodies some of those differences. Yet, at the same time, participants engaging within that discourse would not shy away from difficult discussions, as those conversations have potential not only to disrupt, but also to deeply inform both their own and students' education. In one example, Mary Louise focused the classroom discussion on an article on sexuality (28 March), by telling the students, "Because it's so hard to talk about it, I think we need to talk about it." Henry Giroux (1993) wrote: "Educating for difference, democracy, and ethical responsibility is not about creating passive citizens. It is about providing students with the knowledge, capacities, and opportunities to be noisy, irreverent, and vibrant" (p. 374). And bell hooks (1994) commented that "confronting one another across differences means that we must change ideas about how we learn; rather than fearing conflict we have to find ways to use it as a catalyst for new thinking, for growth" (p. 113). In a poststructural feminist teaching discourse there would be struggle within and toward noisy, irreverent, and vibrant classes to turn conflicts into catalysts for analysis and action.

Second, feminist poststructuralism helped me to understand the possibilities available in deconstructing what is assumed to be "normal" within classroom differences. By encouraging and relying upon differences among classroom participants, the normal becomes complex and problematized. Gloria told her class (15 February), "When you never have to think about your culture, it's like you don't have one. . . . Everyone else has culture and I'm just normal." Some of those engaging within feminist teaching in this research struggled to identify a variety of cultures, thereby disrupting the idea that any one is more normal than others. A poststructural feminist teaching discourse highlights and grapples with conceptions of normalcy as presented in a variety of discourses and dichotomies that affect educational practices.

Finally, feminist poststructural teaching discourse problematizes the idea that there can ever be one singular approach to understanding difference in educational experience. Rather, this discourse would suggest, approaches should be continually reevaluated—the discourse should be left open. As Elizabeth Ellsworth (1992) asserted,

> The terms in which I can and will assert and unsettle "difference" and unlearn my positions of privilege in future classroom practices are wholly

dependent on the Others/others whose presence—with their concrete experiences of privileges and oppressions, and subjugated or oppressive knowledges—I am responding to and acting within any given classroom. (p. 115)

As in many other parts of this analysis, I learned here that in a poststructural feminist teaching discourse there is value in finding tentative solutions and approaches to difference in concert with others who participate in educational experiences.

CHAPTER 8

Powers of Language:
Interrogating Silence and Speech

Silence. A sound. A word. A motion. Silence. Passionate words. Passionate thoughts. Passionate silence. Silence communicates sometimes just as loudly as words. In and outside of educational environments, both silences and speech hold great potential for communicating and learning with each other.

One of my assumptions as a student taking my first women's studies class (one that presumably incorporated feminist approaches to teaching and learning) was that I would feel more comfortable speaking in situations offered there than I had in my other academic work. It was not uncommon for me, as a student, to sit in classrooms, thoroughly engaged, with voices clashing and clamoring for expression inside my head, and yet remain silent for a day, a week, a semester. There were about 40 of us in that class and although each meeting was almost entirely composed of discussion, that semester I failed to utter a word. What happened to my need to speak my thoughts into others' hearing? Was my silence an act of resistance, oppression, or something else? Magda Gere Lewis (1993) has suggested that women's silence can be redefined "not as an absence but as a political act" (p. 3). Although I experienced deep dissonance about the form of my participation that semester and willed myself to change the dynamic, I was not able to perceive myself as politically active within that particular classroom struggle.

Recent work has explored the reasons for and meanings behind silences in communication and education and has suggested multiple understandings for these silences (Lewis, 1993; Orner, 1992). Magda Gere Lewis (1993) made communication, and especially women's silences in education, the centerpiece of her recent work. Therein, she suggested that "the potential power of pedagogical practice, whether in the realm of the personal or that of the political, whether inside the

130

academy or out, is its ability to bring people to a point where they care to listen'' (p. 49).

In this section, I explore the uses of language and communication in feminist teaching discourses—how teachers and students bring each other to listen to various types of communication and expression. I question how speech and silence are perceived in feminist education environments and, further, how they communicate meaning and indications of engagement within those environments. I turn first to prescribed aspects of speech and silence, and then consider what I have come to understand as especially powerful words and silences within feminist teaching discourses. Finally, I consider possibilities for language analysis and enactment within poststructural feminist teaching discourse.

PRESCRIBED SPEECH

Some of those working within feminist teaching discourse have espoused and developed behaviors that prescribed speech by students in their classrooms. For various reasons, these teachers believed that the act of participation through speech was integral to students' learning experiences. Many scholars and educators have pointed out problematic aspects and assumptions that inform this requirement. For example, Mimi Orner (1992) said: ''When Anglo-American feminist and critical pedagogues call for students to find and articulate their voice, they presume singular, essential, authentic, and stable notions of identity'' (p. 86). A requirement of speech further implies a power to know others and, in teacher-student relationships, a power to evaluate. As Dennis Carlson (1995) suggested, ''Unlike the formal and legal power of the state over the individual that tended to predominate in the modern era, pastoral power cannot be exercised without knowing the inside of people's minds, without exploring their souls, without making them reveal their innermost secrets'' (p. 354). In some sense, then, prescribed speech represents teachers' requests to explore the caverns and tunnels of their students' ''true'' minds.

Several teachers in my study believed that verbal participation in class discussions was crucial to the education intended for their classes. One teacher explained her intention in trying to encourage speech in her classroom. Eileen noted that the classroom arrangement and the act of asking students to speak was an acknowledgment of the power relations between herself and students; yet she believed that it was also an attempt to have people learn to create opportunities to speak in subse-

quent situations where they might not be requested or encouraged to
verbalize their thoughts.

> Through the act of going around the room again [asking each per-
> son to speak, it] is in a way, [a] . . . foregrounding of the operating
> in this situation of unequal power. And I have power to make you
> speak and demand your speech at this moment. But also . . . I fan-
> tasize perhaps that if you impose a regularity on it, then it has a dif-
> ferent weight too. Some of it is just the rhythm. [Students think]:
> "OK, it's time now. You made me open my mouth, which I'm go-
> ing to be in the habit of." . . . [I'm] turning it into not a choice of
> being able to not hear [students'] voice[s] again.

Eileen also attempted to teach students to have a certain responsibility
to themselves for speech in the classroom. Through an attention to
students' own comfort levels and possibilities for growth, she brought
to the forefront yet another aspect of student voice:

> Nobody is allowed to be silent in my classroom. Which means that
> I take away from them the power and the burden to decide
> whether or not they need to talk. I take this whole discourse of the
> move to speak or [being] empowered to speak or compelled to
> speak right out of their hands, and throw it, in a sense, back into
> this place of institutional power. Everyone talks and everyone talks
> relatively equally in any given class period. Not completely equally
> but pretty damn close. . . . What that means is that probably for a
> certain group of people in the class, over a period of like 16 weeks,
> they have been terrified to come to class because they know I'm go-
> ing to make them talk. But looking back on the semester, what they
> have is this accumulated sense of having spoken. That fact of hav-
> ing spoken, of having practiced speaking, of having performed the
> act of themselves of speakers, which was not in their previous expe-
> rience, is part now of their repertoire.

Eileen validated the requirement of speech for students in her classrooms by suggesting that she hoped to use her institutionally granted
power to "force" students to develop a "sense of having spoken." She
encouraged students to use their voices and, through that exercise, to
see themselves as verbal participants in other contexts.

Other teachers prescribed speech as well. Their motivations, however, for requiring speech in their classrooms varied greatly. For instance,

several teachers talked about a need to learn from all classroom participants and, in turn, stressed the importance of student speech. As Tonika said,

> I want to hear and everybody else wants to hear what everybody
> else had to say. I will add to it; I will elaborate on what [students]
> say, but I don't want to do that. [Class members] are going to have
> to be just as much a part of this as I am.

Sarah believed that her evaluation of classroom participation (which
included students' participation in the form of speech) took on a different function. In describing this evaluation process, she explained her
rationale in response to student complaints:

> People who complained about [my evaluation of their class partici-
> pation] the most are people who don't like to speak in a group and
> who are uncomfortable with the fact that I give a grade for things
> like in-class presentation because they say they don't feel comfort-
> able speaking in front of a group. And I have to explain over and
> over—and this is in particular for undergraduates—that I'm trying
> to give everybody a chance to have their contribution valued.

Sarah valued classroom speech among other types of evaluation processes because she felt that it provided students with an opportunity to
have their work valued in multiple ways.
    "Finding one's voice" has been understood, in some respects, to
be a liberatory experience. Julie emphasized that participating verbally
in class discussion is important in feminist educational environments.
Yet she described a poignant example of the difficulties that she had in
her classes when she attempted to enact this practice:

> I think most people would think that in a feminist classroom,
> you've got to try to have discussion. What I often do is have them
> do work in groups of two or something for a few minutes and then
> just have a class discussion on what points came up. I have to tell
> you the only reason I do that is to model it. I've observed other
> teachers and consistently it's a waste of time. But that's a contradic-
> tion for me because I think it shouldn't be. . . . A couple weeks
> ago I . . . had everybody working in groups of two. And some peo-
> ple weren't participating. . . . So basically, about one minute in, I
> said, "OK, everybody who has a newspaper either find a partner

to work with or you should leave.'' And then they hate me. So it's real hard.

Many other teachers have shared Julie's difficulty in deciding when and where prescribed and evaluated classroom speech is either necessary or helpful.

PRESCRIBED SILENCE

In certain classroom situations, there was also a contested practice that I term *prescribed silence*. bell hooks (1994) has discussed this concept, describing the prescribed silences inherent in the idea of classrooms as safe places. In her words, ''Many professors have conveyed to me their feeling that the classroom should be a 'safe' place; that usually translates to mean that the professor lectures to a group of quiet students who respond only when they are called on'' (p. 39). Paradoxically, if safety is interpreted as student silence, attempts to establish safety will undoubtedly prescribe environments in which students do not feel safe to speak.

However, many other rationales supported the adherence to a practice that prescribed certain silences. For example, several teachers talked about their desires to have student silence when they were speaking so that they could keep the class ''focused'' on the current topic, usually of the teachers' choosing. The expectation of silence on the part of students was sometimes explicitly stated, as when Kathy loudly proclaimed as she walked into the room, ''Why don't you all stop talking when I start talking?'' Other times, it was not quite as direct, but still conveyed the expectation of silence, as when Kathy explained to her class that she disliked the term *political correctness*. As I heard her tell students, ''I despise the term. I don't care if I ever hear it again. That's a hint not to use it in this class. . . . The charge of 'PC' stops debate—it stifles dialogue.'' The use of the term politically correct was not accepted in this class, apparently because it mitigated against other voices being heard. Ironically, Kathy seemed caught in a tension between prescribing silence on certain topics and ensuring that free and volitional speech would be possible.

More interesting, perhaps, was a different kind of prescribed silence to which only a few teachers alluded. This silence was required when the speaking of certain words and about certain ideas was perceived to be harmful to teachers' goals for the class. Most often, a silence was required when speech would be prejudicial against certain groups of people. For example, Eileen said:

> It's my job to, as great an extent as it's possible, . . . to make the classroom as safe a setting as is possible, given that we are still in culture. . . . I say: "Racism has no place in this classroom. Sexism has no place in this classroom. And to the extent that you know that is your deliberate intention, take it elsewhere. To the extent that you fail to do things [or do things] you didn't intend, we'll work on those things here." Many, many people in my department think this is very controversial. And many other people who think of themselves as feminist call what I do censorship.

Eileen explained her position further:

> I don't believe in censorship in the world per se. In the classroom, I believe in it very much. . . . And it has to do with thinking of a [class] as a kind of a hothouse. . . . It's a hothouse in which you get your flowers grown fast. That means everything is a little more volatile and a little bit heated up and a little bit more in close contact. It means that you can't have noxious fumes to one plant being emitted by the other plant and have them both grow. So you sort of limit what can go on in that particular hothouse in a way that you hope will maximize the growth potential of all the plants that have to be in the room. So it's like a nonsmoking regulation is what I would say. . . . It doesn't say, "You should never ever smoke." It says, "You can't smoke in this room because I'm breathing the same air." So it's not going to level the playing field between the men and the women in my class, but it is going to say, "This is a place where women that are in this group don't have to look at from their peers the same sense of intimidation that they see in the media every day."

In very similar terms, Mary Louise discussed her understandings of topics that she would not accept in her classrooms:

> I guess I think I'm the ultimate responsible person in the room, both for the safety of people to say what they are thinking, but also to let people know there are boundaries here. Not everything is open for statement. So for example, I would not allow openly racist things to be said. I'd be very disturbed. And I would have to say:

"I have some marked boundaries here that can't be crossed, so you can certainly think those things, and you could even talk with me about them in private, but you couldn't say things about people of color, or gays or lesbians in that you could not speak disparagingly based on some dimension of a person." . . . People could certainly question [and] say, "I've been wondering about this and this and this." . . . I know that some people might read this as political correctness, but I don't think so. I think it's respect for [others] in the classroom. So I'm not out to change someone's thinking, but I would hope that people would rethink some of the roots of why they have [a certain] perspective by being in my class. . . . To say openly racist or homophobic things, things that are disparaging to a particular social class or language background, those are not acceptable for me.

Both Eileen and Mary Louise spoke strongly about their beliefs that limiting certain speech in classrooms is not only acceptable, but desirable and perhaps necessary, to foster the most productive learning and growth of all who engage in feminist educational environments.

POWERFUL SPEECH

As seen by the types of speech that were either required or forbidden above, there is certainly speech that some teachers in this study perceived to be either desirable or harmful. Whether for educational or interpersonal reasons, silence and speech were strong considerations for participants in this study. In this section, I turn to viewpoints of especially powerful speech expressed in these feminist classrooms. By powerful speech, I mean speech that seemed, to me, to shape classroom discourse in a way that had strong implications for the experiences participants were able to have and construct. I concentrate on specific incidents that were particularly poignant in explaining moments of powerful speech of both students and teachers. While there were myriad examples that teachers discussed or I observed, I concentrate here on six particular situations, each of which problematizes communication in a unique context.

The first example that I discuss here explores the belief that critical and politically useful speech was powerful. In her class, Danielle struggled to encourage students to feel competent in engaging critically with class material. She recalled this experience in her interview with me:

It takes a while to get students going to the point where they feel enabled in the discussion. But eventually, to varying degrees of success, we get there, and the class becomes increasingly engaged. And I always know that it has really taken off when one of the students gets outraged about something. [A student will say,] "This is really bad! Who funded this anyway?" And I realize that they feel they're entitled to criticize.

Danielle stated further: "The challenge of the course is getting them to recognize that yeah, they have a lot to say about it. And that they're perfectly capable of understanding and, in fact, it's politically important that they understand." Danielle believed it was very important that students learned and assumed the role of critical analysts when presented with content both inside and outside the classroom. She further believed that developing this type of critical and political speech was an important educational process.

As discussed in chapter 6, teachers encouraged critical examination of content brought to the class through a variety of sources. The speech involved in critical examination often proved to be powerful and simultaneously very difficult. Even when ideas were highly contradictory, some teachers nevertheless encouraged their students to engage with and talk about them in classes. Kathy related one highly charged incident where many students expressed anger at one student who had voiced racist remarks in a class. Kathy told me:

The class got so angry at her, calling her racist and this and that. . . . "How can you say that in class?" is what they were asking her. And I said: "She can say that in class because I asked her. I asked all of you to say that. To say something like this—so don't take your anger out on her, when in fact, your anger is about the fact that this fear exists and let's talk about it."

Difficult speech, such as that about racism and sexism, resulted in classroom conflicts at times. However, these same moments of speech, and the tensions that they caused, were seen by Kathy as opportunities to move educational discussions and analyses to different planes and were thus considered to be powerful moments of speech.

Other teachers sought to delineate the "proper" language to use with professors, and believed that disrespectful, as well as respectful, speech (as primarily defined by teachers) was powerful. In one case,

Rosa discussed an incident where she was hurt by what she perceived to be disrespectful speech from her students. As she described it,

> I still think most of us are fighting . . . the socialization of . . . wanting to be liked or wanting to be nurturing. And if you're not fighting that, you're fighting some other sort of battle with a cultural stereotype of what women ought to be. I still struggle with that one. I thought I was over it, and I was teaching last spring, and I don't really care what my students call me. I usually say, since I've gotten older, [students should call me] Professor or Doctor, but if they call me Rosa, it's no big deal if it's done in a respectful way. And two students called me Rosa aggressively as a mark of their hostility in the class. I just was infuriated by it. It wasn't that they broke down this assumed boundary. It was that they did it with a kind of aggression. . . . I didn't want to show my anger about it in class. On the other hand, I wanted to make it clear that wasn't acceptable behavior. And sometimes students just call me that because they're friendly and want that relationship and that's great. But sometimes they do it out of a sense of challenge and that's not OK. So I struggle with that.

In this case, because of her perceptions of hostility, Rosa deemed these students' use of overly personal language to be disrespectful. This speech was powerful enough to "infuriate" her. This powerful language was against the institutional norms of communication that Rosa had come to expect in this classroom environment.

Closely related to the experience that Rosa had was a time that Sarah described when she felt the power of students' speech shaped both her discourse and that of the classroom in a way with which she was uncomfortable. Powerful speech, in this incident, was that which refused to acknowledge positions and opinions of others because of its overbearing presence. Sarah described ongoing classroom communication in one class:

> There are times that I wished that I'd just decided to hold the power for myself, because it would be easier. . . . I've had a couple of people who have been highly verbal—combative at times. And I've constantly tried to balance their right to speak with other people's rights to have time and space as well. And also time for me. And that's a constant struggle. My goal is that . . . all the students would always feel comfortable to ask any question that they wanted to ask either in or out of class. And that the group would

be strong enough that people would really support [beliefs] from a variety of different individuals in the class.

While Sarah's goal was to create space and opportunity for all students in the classroom, the powerful speech of others who monopolized those opportunities made the attainment of this goal very difficult. Speech that disrupted teachers' and other students' participation in classrooms was seen as powerful in shaping classroom experiences for all participants.

Another type of powerful speech related to the idea of authority, difference, and language. Kelly described her difficulty in trying to establish her views of the importance of language and speech when in conflict with students in her class who held certain identity statuses. She described several situations in which her speech and underlying beliefs were contested and problematized because of students' and her own identities. In Kelly's words,

> Sometimes these things are hard to negotiate, this allowing for differences. I do feel quite strongly that language very much shapes the way we perceive ourselves and the world, and that social change occurs in part through language as we describe it. . . . I find it difficult when somebody of a different social identity . . . a person of color makes a statement drawing on her/his experience, that I find troubling. That's a difference that I often grapple with in the classroom. For instance, I'll give you an example in this discussion of mankind and how language doesn't matter. [Some students said]: . . . "What's wrong with calling adult females 'girls'? I don't have any problem with that." And people give me all these examples. And I said, "Well, what about the word nigger?" And I could see students about to respond, "Well, that's different." What I was going to try to point out and get them to see is that yes, our attitudes and values about language change through time, through historical periods. Words intrinsically don't have any value except whatever we assign to them. But I had a student who spoke up about that point and said: "There's nothing wrong with that word. I know lots of Black people who use that word all the time." Now that was very hard to respond to because he was the only African American in the classroom. So those sorts of things are difficult to deal with.

The speech of this particular student, because of his social identity, provided him with an authority in the minds of other students, as well as in Kelly's mind, to speak about the use of certain language. His speech on this subject was powerful.

A final type of speech that played out in powerful ways in classrooms was that which was deemed to be radical or nontraditional. Brianne said that although she wanted to create open and "free-flowing" classrooms, her underlying assumptions supported the opening of space primarily for radical students:

> On one hand, I want to say sort of abstractly that I think classrooms should be open spaces where ideas flow freely. But practically, what I'm thinking of is creating spaces where radical students can think out loud and practice being radical.

Brianne then discussed a specific incident where this radical expression took place. As she described it,

> There was some problematic about people on the Left or feminists or whoever thinking about language carefully or reminding themselves to pay attention to what they are saying or how representations are being constructed. I think there was something problematic and potentially boring about that, but it's so useful in so many situations where it actually works for people in real concrete ways. To see a lesbian in the class confronting homophobia in someone's statement, just to see the reactions to that and see who is able to hear her and who is not [is] in some sense a really positive thing, even if that comes from knee-jerk political correctness.

Brianne defined powerful speech, in this incident, to be that which was spoken by radical students who attempted to expand the boundaries of traditional and stereotypical discourse.

Many types of speech were powerful or pivotal in the feminist classrooms of the teachers participating in this research. Danielle discussed powerful speech as being that which was critical and politically useful. Kathy believed that powerful speech was that which engaged with difficult topics that, on occasion, created classroom conflict. Rosa believed that students' speech was powerful in negative ways when they did not remain within norms of respectability. And Sarah believed that speech that refused to acknowledge the positions, opinions, and voices of others was also powerful. Kelly asserted that powerful speech could be attached to the speaker and her or his identity. Finally, Brianne believed that powerful speech in her classrooms was speech that was radical or nontraditional. The words spoken here did indeed take on a life of their own, exposing culturally embedded expectations and norms of communication that alternately disrupted, redefined, and reinforced "appropriate" speech in feminist classrooms.

POWERFUL SILENCE

Just as speech was powerful at specific moments in classroom discourses, so too could silence be understood to have powerful meanings. As Magda Gere Lewis (1993) asserted, "We need, as well, to hear both the voices *and* the silence through which women engage our social world; to make meaning not only out of what woman [*sic*] say, but also out of what women refuse to say and to understand why we might refuse to speak" (p. 41). Both words and silences convey meanings that have the potential to be powerful in educational environments. In this section, I describe ways that participants in these classrooms conceptualized powerful meanings both of their own and others' silences.

Some teachers saw as powerful the act of remaining silent to allow students to maintain or achieve a greater control of what and how they were learning in a given situation. They acknowledged that it was often helpful for them to remain silent and let students take control of and determine the next course of action for themselves. Kathy put it this way:

> One of the things that I try never to do is to disrupt when students are engaging each other. I try not to disrupt—or actually inject anything if I think it's going along well. Because as soon as you say something as a teacher, it sort of brings a dead end to the discussion.

Kathy told me of a poignant situation in class where two students were challenging each other to expand their viewpoints. She explained her decision to not actively participate in that situation:

> I could actually stand back and sort of watch this engagement happen. So I think it really strengthens me as a teacher to see those kinds of conflicts. There's always the danger that something could get real ugly, but that's the chance I take. I would much rather have had that happening than having them sitting there in their seats taking notes in class.

Tonika even encouraged students to expect her silence in given situations. In her words, "I want to help people to learn how to think. But I can't teach them to learn how to think about it if I tell them what they have to think." From observations and interviews, I learned that several teachers felt that it was appropriate to remain silent during certain situations so that students could control the course of discussion and develop their own thinking. Teachers' own silences were powerful for student learning.

Rae described how she created an environment where both she and some of the more orally active students would learn to be silent. She did this so that those who were less comfortable speaking quickly in a group would be encouraged and enabled to speak:

> [I tell the class]: "We have a responsibility as a group for everybody to have a chance to say. Some people, it just takes them longer." . . . So then I can say, "OK here, some people just need a little bit more time, so what I'm going to try to do is get us to pause a little bit." . . . So that has been a really useful way again to build the sense of, "We are in this together" and to get people to see how their participation and the way they participate affect other people.

Rae believed that silences were powerful when they created spaces in which those who were perhaps less verbal could speak.

Eileen spoke of another type of powerful silence that was manifested in the choices of speech and silence in her classroom. Eileen is a teacher who insisted on mandating student participation through speech in the educational environments that she constructed. And yet she discussed the idea that learning to be silent is also a lesson taught through prescribed speech:

> Learning to have a little bit of power in this situation where you feel that you have less than you might have eventually is also about learning to protect yourself. It's about learning not to, because you are asked to speak, . . . reveal what you are most vulnerable about. So it's also about learning to *not* say. So I think that there are very complicated negotiations that must also be used, every time that [students] open their mouths, about what it was that they were thinking that they aren't going to share with us right now. . . . I do not expect of my students that they reveal to me their emotional material vis-à-vis the classroom.

Eileen saw the silence in not disclosing certain personal topics that would potentially lead students into vulnerable positions as powerful and useful in her classrooms. She pushed, however, to further problematize student silences, particularly women's, because of the social devaluation of their words: "The question, 'Is [what I have to say] important enough?' is so key because . . . people's own baggage about their own unimportance culturally, women's baggage particularly, [makes them wonder], 'Is anything I have to say important enough, ever?'"

Gloria interpreted silence in many ways, suggesting that it can be both a learning style or preference and a weapon used against the teacher and her practices. She explained her evolving understandings of student silences:

> I often thought that when my students were silent, they just didn't know—they didn't have the information—they didn't have anything to say so they were just quiet. But as I began to read their journals and actually reflect on . . . teaching . . . I'm becoming increasingly convinced that [students] use their silence as a weapon—as a way to not engage in the classroom, or have this discussion, so you just get up there and do it on your own.

While in other comments, she expressed a belief that students could engage with classroom content and discourse without speaking, she showed a concern here as well with the uses of students' silences as weapons of resistance against her and the resulting classroom discourses that were being created.

Silence, as speech, can be educationally powerful. In this research, several teachers felt it appropriate to remain silent at times so that students could develop their own thoughts and beliefs before hearing those of the teacher. Rae believed that silences were powerful when they created spaces within which others could speak and explore their ideas. Eileen believed that silence was powerful when chosen to avoid exposing topics about which students felt uncomfortable. And Gloria thought that students' silences could also be used as a weapon of resistance. Silences had powerful meanings and implications for learning and personal safety in some of the discourses that were created in these classrooms.

EMERGING PRACTICES AND CRITIQUES OF LANGUAGE

If I have to stop fighting just to be here, what is it that I want to say?

(Eileen)

In this chapter I considered multiple tensions that surrounded the presences and absences of speech and silence in feminist classrooms. Through discussions of prescribed and powerful speech and silence, I highlighted the often contradictory ways that various forms of communication were understood in these contexts. I turn now to ways that poststructural feminist teaching discourse could work within tensions caused by these contradictions.

First, feminist poststructural teaching discourse encourages multiple forms of participation in education. Rather than valuing only speech or silence, it recognizes a variety of meanings and expressions conveyed in both. For example, Rae said:

> I lay out participation as a piece of what is expected. We talk about ways that we can participate, different ways. I mean it isn't as if everybody has got to be speaking all the time. But active listening, coming to class [is important]. . . . I also say this would be the boringist class in the world if I'm here being responsible for your entertainment and learning.

Mary Louise commented in class (25 April) that "I think people learn best when they feel safe and they can talk both inside and outside of the group." Still, she did not assume that when persons did not speak in her classes, it necessarily meant that they were not engaging with class material and participating in a useful way.

A poststructural feminist teaching discourse considers communication, and learning that takes place during that communication, as the responsibility of *both* teachers and students. When responsibility for learning and communicating is blurred in this way, the onus on students to be silent recipients of knowledge and powerful speech is removed. The responsibility to be knowledge negotiators, rather than solely knowledge "providers" or "takers," is distributed among class participants.

Several teachers discussed their methods of disrupting roles and taking joint responsibility for students' communication in their classrooms. Tonika described her experiences:

> There were classes I took as a graduate student where I never opened my mouth. And I understand why students don't open their mouths sometimes. And I hope I don't penalize people for not opening their mouths, but . . . the classes that I never spoke in, nobody ever tried to get me to speak. Nobody ever tried to figure out [why I didn't speak]. [Perhaps they thought]: "Maybe this

person is shy. Maybe this person just doesn't feel comfortable or capable in this particular class." And what I try to do is to break down those kind of defenses against not talking.

Mary Louise also discussed the "co-responsibility" that she took for students' learning in her classes. In describing an international student who had written in a journal that she felt mute in class, Mary Louise conveyed her approach:

> I was reading her journal and writing back to her, and I said to her that I thought I was partially responsible for her muteness. . . . There have to be ways I can help this very talented thinker speak to the class. . . . So I suggested to her that she come and talk to me about ways that I, in the future, could help. . . . It's not her responsibility alone to speak. There has to be an environment that enables her to speak.

Both Tonika and Mary Louise considered that classroom communication was the co-responsibility of students and teachers.

Finally, in a poststructural feminist teaching discourse, power relations involved in speaking and silence and in attempts to prescribe others' speech or silence would be recognized. Paying attention to communication, in whatever form it took, would be considered valuable and informative. As Jean O'Barr and Mary Wyer (1992) said of students with whom they worked, "If we listen to what these students/contributors say, they thrive on recognition, appreciation, and trust; they notice their marginalization; and they despair of the waste of their talents" (p. 1). Michel Foucault (1984/1988a) suggested his beginning understandings of this power-communication relation as well. In his mind, "common" knowledge framed power as repressive, therefore only limiting speech. To speak, therefore, would be considered to be breaking free from that power, and thus liberatory. Applied to this research, then, student speech would be liberatory and encouraged, perhaps even mandated. Foucault complicated this framework, however, when he insisted that power was primarily productive in its workings. In so doing, he contended that both speech and silence were constructed. Both speech and silence were meaningful and powerful. And, in turn, both speech and silence had the potential to be liberatory and repressive. A poststructural feminist teaching discourse grapples with these tenuous and shifting relations of language in educational environments.

CHAPTER 9

Intersections and Interruptions: Letting Loose with Disruption

The whole point of stories is not "solutions" or "resolutions" but a broadening and even a heightening of our struggles—with new protagonists and antagonists introduced, with new sources of concern or apprehension or hope, as one's mental life accommodates itself to a series of arrivals: guests who have a way of staying, but not necessarily staying put.

(Coles, 1989, p. 129)

Our narration of who we are constructs the new us, not just for the people who are listening but also for yourself.

(Mary Louise Gomez, 14 February)

Thus far, I have told stories about the creation of a feminist teaching discourse whose shaping I both observed and constructed. Although based on the teachers who agreed to take part in my research and on literature that I chose, the interpretations that I present here are my own. In some ways, then, the story that I am beginning to close (for this telling anyway) is a tale of creation, imagination, and playful supposition.

Throughout my constructions, I sought to look at both philosophies and practices or, in Michel Foucault's (1978) words, at strategies and tactics. I attempted to let those two ways of looking at feminist teaching discourse inform and question each other. Through considering both specific and local practices simultaneously with overarching approaches and philosophies, I came to believe that they were interconnected, yet not entirely consonant with each other. The tenuous relations between philosophies and practices, both in myself and in teachers in this research, greatly affected this story.

The spinning of this tale was not without difficulty and "interruptions" in the production. As I was attempting to consider a variety of social forces, philosophies, and enactments of feminist teaching, the voices of others clashed with each other and with my own presuppositions of what this project was to become. At some point, though, the telling of stories must end. In much research, the ending is a summons to action or a grand conclusion about the significance of that particular piece of research. I have, instead, sprinkled my understandings of this research's implications throughout its pages. By doing so, I meant for my meanings and understandings of this work to be taken and exploited by others interested in feminist teaching to the degree that they will serve their purposes.

This leaves me, though, with a final chapter where pressing ideas that have not yet found expression in this work are clamoring for words. Here, then, I focus on my understandings of themes or ideas that evaded the characterization or constriction of categories within which I chose to largely frame this work. Further, by describing the ways in which those broadly construed themes were interrupted and troubled by seemingly disjointed practices, I consider how my story begins to unravel even as it is told. Finally, I conclude with a return to the questions that framed my thoughts as I set out on this journey, not to answer them, but rather to imagine further questions and discourses that they suggest.

CREATING SHARED SPACE

I learned from this research that struggles with understanding power and resistance, knowledge negotiations, differences, and speech and silence were firmly anchored in teachers' desires to create shared teaching and learning spaces in their classrooms. They were trying, as Ruth suggested, to "create a shared imaginative universe."

That phrase is not unproblematic in its implications, however, just as this "shared space" can perhaps never become all that it implies. Creating shared spaces suggests to me a valuing of each other's beings and perspectives, such that the resulting space is relatively equally shaped by all participants. Most of the teachers in this study expressed their desires for that shared space and the corresponding valuing of participants, yet most simultaneously asserted many aspects of their roles and self-expectations generally, before they had met the others with whom they were to create those *shared* spaces. As Brianne suggested to me, she could not imagine a time when she did not have to create the class structure before meeting her students. Although containing an acknowledgment of the lack of understanding that classroom participants can ever hope to have about each other, this generalization of teachers' roles continues to be informed by institutional and social expectations that supersede understandings and implementations not only of the desires of students, but also of teachers' own desires. Shared space is perhaps an impossible but useful goal within many feminist contexts.

Engaging with and planning for a diverse range of classroom activities and knowledge approaches is a beginning in dealing with this dilemma. Being explicit about expectations is as well. Yet the expectations and spectrum of diversity, in this research, largely remained within the scope of teachers' willingness and abilities to explore options that they perceived as being available to their practices. The universe that is being created in these teaching environments was indeed imaginative, and yet as real as any other interactions—all of which have their limitations and restricted visions.

These tensions are inevitable and serve as fuel for continued dialogue and learning. Struggling to craft teaching and learning environments is educationally useful, not in spite of, but because of, the tensions within those efforts. With Harland Bloland (1995), I believe that "in higher education our course is clear. We need to increase and sustain the dialogue, even as we acknowledge that the tension will not, and perhaps should not, be resolved" (p. 554). And while Dennis Carlson (1995) suggested that progress in educational environments is possible, he cautioned, "A democratic progressive discourse in education must always be in the process of being 'made' through an inclusive dialogue on the meaning of progress" (p. 357). Feminist classrooms are not exempt from this need for dialogue on the value, motivations, and implications of their practices.

SOURCES OF DESIRE

Another aspect of this research that spanned the categorical structure I set forth was a sense of desire in teachers' statements and practices. Mary Louise often spoke of her enjoyment in teaching, ending class (21 March) one night by saying, "This was so much fun. I knew I missed something last [week when we didn't meet] and it was you." And Gloria told the class (26 April) that her teaching was driven, at least in part, by feeling, rather than by recipes for "appropriate" practice. In her words, "You can have thousands of recipes and be able to read them all, but it doesn't make you a cook. What makes you a cook is the way you feel about cooking. . . . Being able to read a recipe doesn't make you a better teacher." As I came to understand through interviews and observations, more so than through voices in the literature, laughter and desire were valued highly in much feminist teaching discourse.

This question of desire, however, is seemingly empty without a subsequent phrase or qualification. By this I mean that the question of desire must be in relation to an object, a process, or a relationship. bell hooks (1994) said that for her, "to be changed by ideas was pure pleasure" (p. 3). But resistances between those holding strongly to their own ideological viewpoints and others with divergent, but equally tightly grasped, views lead me to believe that bell hooks's pleasure is not a universal characteristic. As such, I question, What motivates desire in feminist teaching? What are the sources of pleasure? Why do people choose a seemingly often difficult approach to their professions?

Peter McLaren and Colin Lankshear (1993), in addressing the work of Mas'ud Zavarzadeh, contemplated the objects of desire in humanist and poststructuralist pedagogy. In their words:

> Pleasure becomes an experience for containing and subverting the political, yielding a politics of liberation underwritten by "playfulness" and "fancy" which is at odds with bourgeois norms and social practices, but without really *challenging* the social logic of those norms. Liberation becomes a "relief" from the fixity of the social rather than a form of emancipation that comes with seriously challenging existing social relations. The dominant logic is temporarily displaced in an *illusion of freedom*. (p. 403)

They maintained further that

> the pedagogy of poststructuralism is about using "laughter," "parody," "pastiche," and "play" as strategies of subversion which, although they decenter bourgeois relations, do not fundamentally transform them. Such strategies serve merely as a fanciful way of recruiting students into subject positions which maintain existing social relations. (p. 403)

Even these characterizations, however, do not explicitly address and question the quandary about the *sources* of desire in teaching, be it poststructural or feminist.

Liberation has been suggested as a goal of feminist teaching practices; is it also an (unspoken) goal of poststructural teaching? Is desire in feminist teaching the desire to liberate? If so, what are the power relations that this establishes? *Who* is to be liberated, and from what or whom? Is it from the others in our lives who actively or passively constrict and construct our beliefs and options? Or from the structures that exist in our lives that we variously disrupt and support? Is it our desire, with all others, to break entirely free from power relations?

In this research, I learned that many constraints kept students and teachers defined as each other's "Other." While a disruption of those constraints had begun in the practices and beliefs of several teachers in this research, I must wonder, as did Marilyn Frye (1980) more than 15 years ago, about the degree to which others with little interest in the possibilities of feminism (and I will add poststructuralism) have been largely creating feminist and poststructural teaching discourses. In other words, feminist teaching, as situated within a context, has been shaped substantially by that context. There are certainly both points of resistance and of support for current academic and social structures from the feminist teachers in this research. Their desires as well as their identities are multifaceted.

SOCIAL JUSTICE

Through this research, I also learned that feminist teaching discourse was grounded both in a mission of social justice and, in the context of that mission, in finding and creating connections with others, both in and outside classrooms. On a handout that Mary Louise distributed during the second class of the semester, she wrote:

> It is my hope that by making stories of our teaching, we can rethink it; by reading and discussing the stories of others, we can be assisted in being more caring and effective literacy teachers; and that in asking our students to write their stories, and in our listening and responding to these, we can help our students to become more effective writers, that they will take (more) pleasure in reading, and that they will find new links between their worlds outside of school and the possible other worlds both within it and outside it.

These hopes were reinforced throughout interviews and class observations with Mary Louise. For example, in another class (14 February), she said, "Maybe those who've created the borders have as much of a responsibility to cross them as do the ones that they've *othered*." And in a later interview, she told me, "My goal is that my teaching, my research, and my service all serve people who are not served well in this country." Many other teachers in this research also told me about their attempts to create socially just classrooms and to work toward the same in other areas of society.

James Baldwin (1963/1988) suggested in his 1963 address, "A Talk to Teachers" that "the crucial paradox which confronts us here is that the whole process of education occurs within a social framework and is designed to perpetuate the aims of society" (pp. 3–4). This conundrum continues to face education today for those who are seeking to change the processes and practices that maintain "normal" ways of functioning in higher education. Change, and social justice, must be considered as existing in a situation, a context, that has implications for the success or usefulness of that justice. What are the barriers to this mission of social justice? Who will decide what changes are necessary or valuable? Who will define social justice? Can (and should) social justice become an "aim of society"?

Several scholars have addressed and problematized these questions while outlining some of the most difficult items on a social justice agenda (Carlson, 1995; Collins, 1991; hooks; 1984; Luke, 1992). For example, Patricia Hill Collins (1991) suggested that not only must individuals be aware of the ways in which they are oppressed; they must also consider the ways in which they are oppressing others:

> Although most individuals have little difficulty identifying their own victimization within some major system of oppression—whether it be by race, social class, religion, physical ability, sexual orientation, ethnicity, age or gender—they typically fail to see how their thoughts and actions uphold someone else's subordination. Thus white feminists routinely point with confidence to their oppression as women but resist seeing how much their white skin privileges them. (p. 229)

Kathy concurred with this perspective and added:

> I think that when people are forced to look at their own individuality, bereft of privilege, that it leaves some of the impression of what other people go through. It also leaves them with an impression of what may be necessary for true equality and justice in the society. Because a lot of people . . . [say]: "I'm all for justice and everything. But what will I have to give up?" And we talked [in my class] in very real terms about what, in fact, may have to go. What would we have ventured to gain? And I think for some people that's really important and it works. And for others, [they think]: "Hey, this is too much work. I don't want to deal with it." So then people can at least be honest about whether they are interested in change and justice, or not.

Both teachers and students are able to espouse or reject a mission of social justice. While Kathy tried to define in her class what this mission might mean on an individual basis, both the mission and the tactics through which that mission can be supported can (and I believe should) remain open for contextualized redefinition.

bell hooks (1984) believed that a mission of social justice is complicated and impeded by problems of communication and the institutionalization of feminist teaching practices:

> The ability to "translate" ideas to an audience that varies in age, sex, ethnicity, degree of literacy is a skill feminist educators need to develop. Concentration of feminist educators in universities encourages habitual use of an academic style that may make it impossible for teachers to communicate effectively with individuals who are not familiar with either academic style or jargon. (p. 111)

Carmen Luke (1992) believed that it was not only the institutionalization of feminist teaching that hindered what she understood to be a mission of social justice. Rather, she believed that social constraints (that were largely unaffected by feminist educational practices) served to minimize the effects of feminist teachers' intentions. Luke's words are worth quoting at length:

> The point is this: to grant equal classroom time to female students, to democratize the classroom speech situation, and to encourage marginal groups to make public what is personal and private does not alter theoretically or practically those gendered structural divisions upon which liberal capitalism and its knowledge industries are based. Those very divisions have generated countless discourses of, strategies and pleas for "equalities" in the first place. . . . Consider, for instance, that few critically oriented teacher educators would disagree that many students (female or male) are quick to admit to the need for teaching against oppression, for developing and in fact using in classroom dialogue and writing a "language of critique." Many female and male student teachers produce critical self-knowledge and "demonstrate" critical dialectical thinking, a language of critique, and even a pro-feminist stance in the seminar essay and debate. Yet it is women who look after children while studying, miss classes to tend to sick children, and will encounter obstacles to "academic success" by male academics that male students by and large do not confront. . . . They will have to keep their feminist politics in check in order to qualify for tenure and promotion, and to retain their jobs in a patriarchal system that writes their positions and possibilities for them. (pp. 37–38)

The difficulties in implementing this mission of social justice seem endless, as the agenda for change, as Luke defined it, is monumental.

The definitions of social justice varied among the teachers in this research and in literature that I reviewed. Some teachers wished to empower their students, unproblematically asserting that they were to perform a liberatory role. Others wished to retain largely traditional roles, lecturing and empowering—seeking justice—through "giving" their students knowledge. Some teachers tried to enact social justice by mandating speech in their classrooms; others did so by allowing for silences. Julie described her conundrum with and redefinitions of social justice and diversity work. In her words:

> The whole contradiction about how to really meaningfully move forward on diversity, anti-oppression work is one that I suspect I'll spend my life trying to figure out. I don't think we've really found the ways. I think it is such a huge part of what divides people and I would really like to be a part of finding ways of bridging that and moving beyond it. And I don't know if I have. . . . I don't think that anyone who cares about their teaching as much as I do doesn't constantly struggle with it.

Judith Hoover and Leigh Anne Howard's (1995) comments pertained to Julie's struggle, and yet provided a ray of hope for those seeking social justice and equity within a postmodern agenda: "If some versions of postmodernism have suggested no truth, other more hopeful versions suggest multiple truths that could foster multivocal community" (p. 973). Social justice agendas, based on equity and fairness, remain in tenuous relations both with one another and with the practices they seek to rupture.

CONTINUING ON A JOURNEY OF KNOWING

> Without paying particular attention to our specific practices of pedagogy—those which have constructed what we are today and those toward which we aim in our educational and political dreams of different societies—we might altogether overlook the ways in which pedagogy operates, and, furthermore, the pedagogies for which we argue so earnestly and sincerely will remain inconsistent with the pedagogies of our arguments.
>
> (Gore, 1993, p. 157)

The questions that broadly guided this analysis were, What contributes to a multiplicity of forms of feminist teaching? and, How does power influence constructions of feminist teaching? I have discussed how teachers' identities, students, and institutional structures shaped the feminist teaching discourse that I am in the process of learning from and constructing. I have also considered the ways in which power is present through resistances and constructions of power, knowledge negotiations, understandings and enactments of difference, and speech and silence in feminist classrooms. Here, rather than provide a conclusion to this story, I attempt to push the boundaries of my guiding questions and follow, through questioning, paths that I chose not to follow in this particular research, but that I found to be compelling through these experiences.

A question that has intrigued me since early in this study has to deal with feminist learning, not in terms of what teachers should or can do with or for students, but rather in terms of the types of students who are best suited for the kinds of learning situations that feminist teachers attempt to construct. Admittedly, there would not be one "type" of feminist learner, just as there is not one type of feminist teaching. Yet I believe it would be interesting to ask, What types of learners choose to take part in crafting feminist teaching practices or practices with similar characteristics? What are their motivations and intentions? Further, what educational experiences (broadly defined) do different types of learners have both in and as a result of feminist educational environments?

While I have tried, in this analysis, to examine feminist teaching practices through poststructural feminist lenses, the vast majority of these teachers would not claim their teaching to be poststructural. A useful next step in this analysis would be to try to understand explicitly poststructural feminist teaching practices, as well as conditions that they disrupt and by which they are disrupted. Although I have begun to approach this question, the quandaries that are proposed in this research lead me to believe that the discussion is not, and probably never will be, ready for closure.

As to my initial goals for engaging in this endeavor, I have fulfilled them only partially and yet quite satisfactorily. On the one hand, I have not collected the "answers" to my questions, nor have I figured out once and for all how I want to take my place in feminist teaching discourse. On the other hand, I have learned a great deal about struggles and strategies, tensions and turning points, in the work of those who claim some of the same identities to which I aspire. It is my hope that this work will be as useful to others as it was to me in understanding influences on and resulting expressions of a constantly changing feminist teaching discourse, while simultaneously providing options for those wishing to explore new opportunities suggested by poststructural feminism.

Notes

CHAPTER 2

1. In order to preserve confidentiality and yet acknowledge the importance of ethnicity of which these teachers spoke, I removed specific non-White ethnic identifiers and replaced them with "woman of color." While this choice risks placing all non-White women together in an unproblematized category, it helps to prevent the assumption that the experiences of one member of a group are generalizable to all members of that group.

CHAPTER 4

1. For the purposes of this work, and in the interests of confidentiality, *large* is defined as having over 50 students; *midsized* as 25–50 students; and *small* as fewer than 25 students.

CHAPTER 5

1. By using Eileen's and other teachers' words within a context of feminist poststructural teaching discourse, I do not mean to categorize these teachers as existing only within that framework. Rather, I believe that their words and practices can serve to inform my conceptualizations of the possibilities for that discourse.

References

Acker, Sandra. (1987). Feminist theory and the study of gender and education. *International Review of Education, 33,* 419–435.

Alcoff, Linda. (1988). Cultural feminism versus poststructuralism: The identity crisis in feminist theory. In Elizabeth Minnich, Jean O'Barr, & Rachel Rosenfeld (Eds.), *Reconstructing the Academy: Women's education and women's studies* (pp. 257–288). Chicago: University of Chicago Press.

Baldwin, James. (1988). A talk to teachers. In Rick Simonson & Scott Walker (Eds.), *Multicultural literacy: Opening the American mind* (pp. 3–12). Saint Paul, MN: Graywolf Press (Original work published 1963)

Banks, Taunya Lovell. (1997). Two life stories: Reflections of one Black woman law professor. In Adrien Katherine Wing (Ed.), *Critical race feminism* (pp. 96–100). New York: New York University Press.

Bennett, Roberta S. (1991). Empowerment = Work over time: Can there be feminist pedagogy in the sport sciences? *Journal of Physical Education, Recreation, and Dance, 62,* 62–67, 75.

Best, Stephen, & Doug Kellner. (1991). *Postmodern theory.* New York: Guilford.

Bloland, Harland, G. (1995). Postmodernism and higher education. *Journal of Higher Education, 66* (5), 521–559.

Boxer, Marilyn J. (1985). Women's studies, feminist goals, and the science of women. In Barbara M. Solomon (Ed.), *In the company of educated women: A history of women and higher education in America* (pp. 184–204). New Haven: Yale University Press.

Bright, Claire. (1987). Teaching feminist pedagogy: An undergraduate course. *Women's Studies Quarterly, 15* (3/4), 96–100.

Bunch, Charlotte. (1983). Not by degrees: Feminist theory and education. In Charlotte Bunch & Sandra Pollack (Eds.), *Learning our way: Essays in feminist education* (pp. 248–260). Trumansburg, NY: Crossing Press.

Burbules, Nicholas. (1986). A theory of power in education. *Educational Theory, 5,* 95–114.

Carlson, Dennis. (1995). Making progress: Progressive education in the postmodern. *Educational Theory, 45* (3), 337–357.

Coles, Robert. (1989). *The call of stories: Teaching and the moral imagination.* Boston: Houghton Mifflin.

Collins, Patricia Hill. (1991). *Black feminist thought: Knowledge, consciousness, and the politics of empowerment.* New York: Routledge, Chapman & Hall.

Deay, Ardeth, & Judith Stitzel. (1992). Reshaping the introductory women's studies course: Dealing up-front with anger, resistance, and reality. *Feminist Teacher, 6* (1), 29–33.

Dewar, Allison. (1991). Feminist pedagogy in physical education: Promises, possibilities, and pitfalls. *Journal of Physical Education, Recreation, and Dance, 62,* 68–77.

Dunn, Kathleen. (1993). Feminist teaching: Who are your students? *Women's Studies Quarterly, 21* (3/4), 39–45.

Eichhorn, Jill, Sara Farris, Karen Hayes, Adriana Hernandez, Susan C. Jarratt, Karen Power-Stubb, & Marian M. Sciachitano. (1992). A symposium on feminist experiences in the composition classroom. *College Composition and Communication, 43* (3), 297–322.

Ellsworth, Elizabeth. (1992). Why doesn't this feel empowering? Working through the repressive myths of critical pedagogy. In Carmen Luke & Jennifer Gore (Eds.), *Feminisms and critical pedagogy* (pp. 90–119). New York: Routledge. (Original work published 1989)

Ellsworth, Elizabeth. (1993). Teaching to support unassimilated difference. *Radical Teacher, 42,* 4–9.

Fine, Michelle. (1995). Dis-stance and other stances: Negotiations of power inside feminist research. In Andrew Gitlin (Ed.), *Power and method: Political activism and educational research* (pp. 13–35). New York: Routledge.

Flax, Jane. (1993). *Disputed subjects: Essays on psychoanalysis, politics and philosophy.* New York: Routledge.

Foucault, Michel. (1978). *The History of Sexuality: An Introduction.* (Vol. 1). New York: Random House.

Foucault, Michel. (1988a). On power. In Lawrence D. Kritzman (Ed.), *Michel Foucault: Politics, philosophy and cultures: Interviews and other writings 1977–1984* (pp. 96–109). New York: Routledge. (Original work published in 1984)

Foucault, Michel. (1988b). Power and sex. In Lawrence D. Kritzman (Ed.), *Michel Foucault: Politics, philosophy and cultures: Interviews and other writings 1977–1984* (pp. 110–124). New York: Routledge. (Original work published in 1977)

Foucault, Michel. (1988c). Practicing criticism. In Lawrence D. Kritzman (Ed.), *Michel Foucault: Politics, philosophy and cultures: Interviews and other writings 1977–1984* (pp. 153–156). New York: Routledge. (Original work published in 1981)

Fraser, Nancy, & Linda Nicholson. (1988). Social criticism without philosophy: An encounter between feminism and postmodernism. In Andrew Ross (Ed.), *Universal abandon: The politics of postmodernism* (pp. 83–104). Minneapolis: University of Minnesota Press.

Frye, Marilyn. (1980). On second thought. . . . *Radical Teacher, 17,* 37–38.

Frye, Marilyn. (1992a). The possibility of feminist theory. In *Willful virgin: Essays in feminism, 1976–1992* (pp. 59–75). Freedom, CA: Crossing Press.

Frye, Marilyn. (1992b). White woman feminist. In *Willful virgin: Essays in feminism, 1976–1992* (pp. 147–169). Freedom, CA: Crossing Press.

Giroux, Henry. (1993). Literacy and the politics of difference. In Colin Lankshear

& Peter L. McLaren (Eds.), *Critical literacy: Politics, practice, and the postmodern* (pp. 367–378). Albany, NY: State University of New York Press.

Giroux, Jeanne Brady. (1989). Feminist theory as pedagogical practice. *Contemporary Education, 61* (1), 6–10.

Gomez, Mary Louise. (in press). Telling stories of our literacy teaching, reflecting on our practices. In Carl A. Grant & Mary Louise Gomez (Eds.), *Campus and classroom: Making schooling multicultural.* Columbus: Merrill.

Gore, Jennifer. (1990). What we can do for you! What *can* "we" do for "you"?: Struggling over empowerment in critical and feminist pedagogy. *Educational Foundations, 4* (3), 5–26.

Gore, Jennifer. (1993). *The struggle for pedagogies: Critical and feminist discourses as regimes of truth.* New York: Routledge.

Gore, Jennifer M. (1997). *On the use of empirical research for the development of a theory of pedagogy.* Paper presented at the Annual Meeting of the American Educational Research Association.

Grumet, Madeleine R. (1991). The politics of personal knowledge. In Carol Witherell & Nel Noddings (Eds.), *Stories lives tell: Narrative and dialogue in education* (pp. 67–78). New York: Teachers College Press.

Heald, Susan. (1989). The madwoman out of the attic: Feminist teaching in the margins. *Resources for Feminist Research, 18,* 22–26.

hooks, bell. (1984). *Feminist theory from margin to center.* Boston: South End Press.

hooks, bell. (1994). *Teaching to transgress: Education as the practice of freedom.* New York: Routledge.

Hoover, Judith D., & Leigh Anne Howard. (1995). The political correctness controversy revisited: Retreat from argumentation and reaffirmation of critical dialogue. *American Behavioral Scientist, 38* (7), 963–975.

Howe, Florence. (1977). *Seven years later: Women's studies programs in 1976: A report of the National Advisory Council on Women's Educational Programs.* New York: State University of New York Press.

Jipson, Janice. (1995). Teacher-mother: An imposition of identity. In Janice Jipson, Petra Munro, Susan Victor, Karen Froude Jones, & Gretchen Freed-Rowland (Eds.), *Repositioning feminism and education: Perspectives on educating for social change* (pp. 21–36). Westport, CT: Bergin & Garvey.

Kerr, Clark. (1995). *The uses of the university.* Cambridge, MA: Harvard University Press.

Kolodny, Annette. (1988). Dancing between left and right: Feminism and the academic minefield in the 1980s. *Feminist Studies, 14* (3), 453–466.

Lather, Patti. (1991). *Getting smart: Feminist research and pedagogy with/in the postmodern.* New York: Routledge.

Lee, Patricia A. (1994). To dance one's understanding. *Educational Leadership, 51,* 81–83.

Lewis, Magda. (1990). Interrupting patriarchy: Politics, resistance and transformation in the feminist classroom. *Harvard Educational Review, 60* (4), 467–488.

Lewis, Magda Gere. (1993). *Without a word: Teaching beyond women's silence.* New York: Routledge.

Luke, Carmen. (1992). Feminist politics in radical pedagogy. In Carmen Luke & Jennifer Gore (Eds.), *Feminisms and critical pedagogy* (pp. 25–53). New York: Routledge.

Luke, Carmen, & Jennifer Gore. (Eds.). (1992a). *Feminisms and critical pedagogy.* New York: Routledge.

Luke, Carmen, & Jennifer Gore. (1992b). Introduction. In *Feminisms and critical pedagogy* (pp. 1–14). New York: Routledge.

Lusted, David. (1986). Why pedagogy? *Screen, 27* (5), 2–14.

Maher, Frances A. (1985). Classroom pedagogy and the new scholarship on women. In Margo Culley & Catherine Portuges (Eds.), *Gendered subjects: The dynamics of feminist teaching* (pp. 29–48). Boston: Routledge & Kegan Paul.

Maher, Frances A. (1987). Inquiry teaching and feminist pedagogy. *Social Education, 51* (3), 186–192.

Maher, Frances A., & Mary Kay Thompson Tetreault. (1994). *The feminist classroom.* New York: Basic Books.

Makosky, Vivian P., & Michele A. Paludi. (1990). Feminism and women's studies in the academy. In Michele A. Paludi & Gertrude A. Steuernagel (Eds.), *Foundations for a feminist restructuring of the academic disciplines* (pp. 1–37). New York: Haworth.

McLaren, Peter L., & Colin Lankshear. (1993). Critical literacy and the postmodern turn. In Colin Lankshear & Peter L. McLaren (Eds.), *Critical literacy: Politics, practice, and the postmodern* (pp. 379–420). Albany, NY: State University of New York Press.

Middleton, Sue. (1993). *Educating feminists: Life histories and pedagogy.* New York: Teachers College Press.

Middleton, Sue. (1995). Doing feminist educational theory: A post-modernist perspective. *Gender and Education, 7* (1), 87–100.

Morgan, Mary Y., & J. Lyn Rhoden. (1995). Change in white college women's understanding of sexism: Empowerment through critical reflection. *National Women's Studies Association Journal, 7* (2), 35–57.

Munro, Petra. (1996). Resisting "resistance": Stories women teachers tell. *Journal of Curriculum Theorizing, 12* (1), 16–28.

Nicholson, Carol. (1989). Postmodernism, feminism, and education: The need for solidarity. *Educational Theory, 39* (3), 197–205.

Nicholson, Carol. (1995). Postmodern feminisms. In Michael Peters (Ed.), *Education and the postmodern condition* (pp. 75–85). Westport, CT: Bergin & Garvey.

O'Barr, Jean, & Mary Wyer. (1992). *Engaging feminism: Students speak up and speak out.* Charlottesville, VA: University Press of Virginia.

Orner, Mimi. (1992). Interrupting the calls for student voice in "liberatory" education: A feminist poststructuralist perspective. In Carmen Luke & Jennifer Gore (Eds.), *Feminisms and critical pedagogy* (pp. 74–89). New York: Routledge.

Palmer, Parker. (1983). *To know as we are known: A spirituality of education.* New York: HarperCollins.

Pirsig, Robert. (1974). *Zen and the art of motorcycle maintenance.* New York: Morrow.

Rakow, Lana F. (1992). Gender and race in the classroom: Teaching way out of line. *Feminist Teacher, 6* (1), 10–13.

Robinson, Lora H. (1973). *Women's studies: Courses and programs for higher education*. Washington, D.C.: American Association for Higher Education.

Rockhill, Kathleen. (1993). (Dis)connecting literacy and sexuality: Speaking the unspeakable in the classroom. In Colin Lankshear & Peter L. McLaren (Eds.), *Critical literacy: Politics, practice, and the postmodern* (pp. 335–366). Albany, NY: State University of New York Press.

Ropers-Huilman, Becky. (1996). Shaping an island of power and change: Creating a feminist poststructural teaching discourse. Unpublished doctoral dissertation, University of Wisconsin.

Ross, Andrew. (1988). Introduction. In *Universal abandon: The politics of postmodernism* (pp. vii–xviii). Minneapolis: University of Minnesota Press.

Sawicki, Jana. (1991). *Disciplining Foucault: Feminism, power, and the body*. New York: Routledge.

Schniedewind, Nancy. (1983). Feminist values: Guidelines for teaching methodology in women's studies. *Radical Teacher, 18,* 25–28.

Schubert, J. Daniel. (1995). From a politics of transgression toward an ethics of reflexivity: Foucault, Bourdieu, and academic practice. *American Behavioral Scientist, 38* (7), 1003–1017.

Scott, Joan Wallach. (1990). Deconstructing equality-versus-difference: Or, the uses of poststructuralist theory for feminism. In Marianne Hirsch & Evelyn Fox Keller (Eds.), *Conflicts in Feminism* (pp. 134–148). New York: Routledge.

Smith, Lauren. (1994). Secret basketball: One problem with the student-centered classroom. *Feminist Teacher, 8* (1), 16–19.

Swartzlander, Susan, Diana Pace, & Virginia Lee Stamler. (1993, February 17). The ethics of requiring students to write about their personal lives. *The Chronicle of Higher Education,* B1–B2.

Tappan, Mark B., & Martin J. Packer (Eds.). (1991). *Narrative and storytelling: Implications for understanding moral development*. San Francisco: Jossey-Bass.

Tong, Rosemarie. (1989). *Feminist thought: A comprehensive introduction*. San Francisco: Westview.

Wasser, Judith Davidson, & Liora Bresler. (1996). Working in the interpretive zone: Conceptualizing collaboration in qualitative research teams. *Educational researcher, 25* (5), 5–15.

Weedon, Chris. (1987). *Feminist practice and poststructuralist theory*. Oxford: Basil Blackwell.

Weiler, Kathleen. (1988). *Women teaching for change: Gender, class and power*. New York: Bergin & Garvey.

Wieseltier, Leon. (1994, November 28). Against identity. *The New Republic,* 24–32.

Young-Bruehl, Elisabeth. (1988). The education of women as philosophers. In Elizabeth K. Minnich, Jean F. O'Barr, & Rachel Rosenfeld (Eds.), *Reconstructing the academy: Women's education and women's studies* (pp. 9–23). Chicago: University of Chicago Press.

Index

About the Author

Becky Ropers-Huilman is an assistant professor in both the College of Education and the Program of Women's and Gender Studies at Louisiana State University. Her research and interests focus on feminist intersections with institutions of higher education, feminist theory and methodology, higher education cultures, teaching and learning in academic environments, and critical and poststructural approaches to inquiry. Her work has been published in *Gender & Education*, *Feminist Teacher*, and *Higher Education: Handbook of Theory and Research*. Her research on feminist teaching in higher education, as enriched and complicated by poststructural and critical perspectives, provokes much of the writing and thinking she continues to pursue.